*Legacy Edition*

# HOW MUCH FAITH DOES IT TAKE ...
## To Move the Hand of God?

### B. J. Willhite

Hisway Prayer Publications
P. O. Box 762
Jamul, CA 91935

*How Much Faith Does it Take ... To Move the Hand of God?*
*Legacy Edition*

ISBN: 978-1-879545-22-9

Copyright© 2022 by B. J. Willhite

All rights reserved

Printed in the United States of America

Published by Hisway Prayer Publications
P. O. Box 762
Jamul, CA 91935

No part of this book may be reproduced in any form including electronic, mechanical, photocopying without permission in writing from the publisher Hisway Prayer Publications.

Unless indicated all Scripture quotations are taken from the New International Version of the Bible, Copyright© 1978 by New York International Bible Society. Used by permission.

All Quotations from the Amplified Bible, expanded edition are marked AMP. The Zondervan Corporation and Lockman Foundation 1987, Used by permission. All quotations from the Living Bible Paraphrased Reference Edition are marked TLB. Tyndale House Publishers 1980.

Used by permission.

**Publishers Note:**

We all need heroes of the faith. We are very fortunate to have met Pastor Bob Willhite early in our ministry many years ago. Pastor Willhite became both our mentor in prayer and hero of faith. This great man's teachings on the subject of prayer radically impacted our lives and thousands of others throughout the U.S. and Internationally. "How Much Faith Does it Take...to Move the Hand of God?" was written during a remarkable time in history when God was calling His people to prayer. (Ronald Reagan was President; the Berlin Wall was a focus point; and the Cold War was soon to end with the collapse of U.S.S.R.) National Call to Prayer began in Rockwall, Texas 30 + years ago and is still functioning to this day encouraging people to pray.

This book is one of several Legacy editions published to honor and perpetuate Pastor Willhite's great revelations on prayer that can be life-changing to the reader. It is a compilation of manuscripts* produced from Pastor Willhite teaching the principles of prayer in conferences and churches that made a significant difference in his life and the lives of the many thousands worldwide. These truths give the common, ordinary believer the courage to pray with great expectation knowing God has heard their prayers and all of heaven is working in their behalf. (*manuscripts adapted for the reader's ease)

## Repetition on Purpose

Portions of this material will be reoccurring in different chapters. Please bear in mind that the goal of this book is to capture the very essence of Pastor Bob Willhite's heart for impartation.

Our reprinting of these inspiring books is to leave a Legacy of this great man's prayer teachings. You probably have never heard these principles of prayer anywhere else. They will encourage you, build your faith, and answer many of the questions you have had about prayer. You can listen to Pastor Bob's teaching at Hisway School of Prayer on most of the popular podcast platforms. Our prayer is that you will answer the call to prayer as we and thousands of others have.

One of the first principles that we learned from Pastor Bob was: "If you have enough faith to pray...you have enough faith to move the hand of God".

God Bless You,
John & Kathy Casto
Hisway Prayer Publications

# About the Author

B. J. Willhite was born in northwest Arkansas in the days of the old tri-state Pentecostal camp meetings and grew up under the preaching of men of God like Donald Gee and Raymond T. Richey. As a boy he saw platforms littered with crutches, braces, and wheelchairs and heard the joyful testimonies of the people who no longer needed them. Both of his parents were faithful praying people. His mother literally died on her knees while in prayer, and his aunt died in the same manner.

At the age of nineteen, B. J. Willhite fully committed his life to the Lord and to prayer. Hungry to know God, he often prayed from the conclusion of the Sunday morning service until time for the Sunday evening service to begin. Military service did not weaken his prayer life. His habit of beginning every day with prayer continued. In 1947 he married, and began preaching in 1949. Pastor Willhite recalls, "I knew that preachers, of all people, should pray: therefore, I set myself to develop more discipline in prayer than ever before." And pray he did, all through the twenty-eight years he pastored churches in Oklahoma, Missouri, Arkansas, and Texas.

In January of 1979, Pastor Willhite had just arisen from his knees and sat down at his desk when he heard the beginning of a radio broadcast – without the aid of a radio. He listened in amazement as a booming bass voice sang the theme song, "God of Our Fathers." Next, the opening announcements were made, and the program began. At that moment the concept of a 300,000 member prayer army crystallized in his mind – an army that must be enlisted, instructed, inspired, and encouraged to pray through a national call to prayer. That vision became the driving force in his life.

# Dedication

*To Velma, my wife and prayer partner for over Seventy years.*

# Table of Contents

Section One: The Booklet ................................................................. 1

    Introduction: The Purpose Of Prayer ............................... 3

    Chapter One: Faith To Obey ............................................. 5

    Chapter TwoFaith To Pray ............................................... 11

    Chapter Three: Faith To Stay Persistent When God Is Silent ............................................................................... 17

    Chapter Four: Faith To Walk On Your Doubts ................ 23

Section Two: The Manuscripts ....................................................... 29

    Morning Prayer Conference ............................................. 31

    National Call To Prayer Conference ................................ 71

    Pastors Conference ........................................................... 91

# SECTION ONE
# THE BOOKLET

**Publishers Note:**

The following section contains the original manuscript of the small booklet Pastor Willhite wrote covering this teaching.

# Introduction
# The Purpose of Prayer

Prayer is more than a maintenance program or a good idea. You see, everything in this universe operates by divine law and established principle, and that is the way it will be unless there is a reason for it to be otherwise. This is where prayer comes in.

Why do we pray? We pray because **prayer is the means by which God is justified in divinely intervening in any given situation. If we do not pray, the situation will follow its natural course.**

You see, God has a divine will about anything that makes any difference in this universe. Therefore, we must find the divine will and pray it. Agreeing with Him that His will shall be done.

We must know His will and declare it in prayer. I believe that is the central thought in John 14:13 when Jesus pledged, "And whatsoever ye shall ask in my name, that will I do, that the Father may be glorified in the Son." After much study and prayer, this is the way I would paraphrase that verse:

*Whatsoever you ask* by **My command and authority, acting in My behalf for the advancement of My Kingdom,** *I will do it that the Father may be glorified in the Son.*

It is vital that we understand this very important point. It is not that *we* wait for God, but that *He* waits for us to come into agreement with His will and to speak it in prayer.

Remember: Prayer is not twisting God's arm in order to make Him do what He does not want to do. Prayer is finding God's divine will, coming into agreement with it, and declaring that His will shall be done in the situation. As we learn to find God's will and pray it, we become instruments in the hand of God through which He can implement His will in our generation.

Now that we've talked about *why* we pray, let's examine four power-packed principles that will *keep* us praying even when we are weary and discouraged and wonder, "Will my prayer make a difference? Do I have enough faith to move the hand of God?"

# Chapter One
# Faith to Obey

If a reporter from the NBC Nightly News poked a microphone in your face and asked, "Do you believe God answers prayer?" you would probably square your shoulders, look right n the camera, and confidently affirm: "Yes, I most certainly do." That's what I'd say anyway, and I think most Christians would agree with me.

But, most believers aren't asking the question, "Does God answer prayer?" Instead, they're perplexed by thoughts like this: "Will God hear *me*? Will God answer *my* prayer? I know it takes faith to get answers to prayer, and I'm not sure I have enough faith." Am I right? Have you ever carried on that conversation with yourself? If so, then you're just the person I want to talk to about this illusive, intangible thing called "faith."

The Scriptures seem to affirm that diligent, earnest, intent seeking God is the greatest expression of faith. If you really do have faith, you will diligently seek God. If you do not have faith in your heart, you will *not* diligently seek God. Consider Hebrews 11:6: *"But without faith it is impossible to please Him; for he that cometh to God must believe that He is, and that He is a rewarder of them that diligently seek Him."* We know by this verse that it takes faith to move the hand of God. The problem is that we are not sure just how much faith it takes. I want to prove that you have enough faith to move the hand of God because when you believe that, you will diligently pray.

If we're going to talk about faith, perhaps we should make a quick survey of what the Scriptures say in regard to faith. We know that faith comes by hearing (Romans 10:17), and that God gives every man a measure of faith (Romans 12:3). There are different qualities and quantities of faith; *weak* faith (Romans 14:1), *no* faith (Mark 4:40), *full* of faith (Acts 6:5), *unfeigned* faith (2 Timothy 1:51), etc.

The disciples prayed, *"Increase our faith,"* (Luke 17:5). We know that faith can *grow* (2 Thessalonians 1:3), and that it can be *seen* (Matthew 9:2, Mark 2:5). The Apostles spoke of people who were *steadfast* in faith (Colossians 2:5), *established* in faith ( Colossians 2:7), *sound* in faith (Titus 1:13), *rich* in faith (James 2:5), etc. And God Himself is the Author and Finisher of our faith (Hebrews 12:2). We would all agree that there is much to learn about faith.

But where are you and I in all this? Do we really have enough faith to move the hand of God, or are we simply wasting our time when we try to pray? Will our prayers make any difference? I want to share four vital power principles from Scripture that I believe will enable you to understand that you *do* have enough faith to move the hand of God. These four truths can enable you to become diligent I prayer and receive answers to your petitions. And now, if you are ready, let's turn our attention to principle number one.

The story in Luke 5:1-8 is a familiar one; in fact, it is so familiar I'm afraid we may" have missed one of its most important teachings.

A great crowd of people had followed Jesus to the Sea of Galilee early one morning where two fishing boats had come to shore, and the fishermen were washing their nets after a long night's toil. Jesus approached one of the fishermen, Simon Peter, and asked if Simon would thrust his boat out a little distance from land allow Him to sit in it and teach people on shore. Peter willingly obliged. But when the teaching was over and Jesus commanded, "Launch out into the deep and let down your net for a draught (Luke 5:4), the weary fisherman balked. After all, he and his partners had fished this lake for years. They knew when the fish were running and when they weren't, and they had just completed a night of back-breaking toil and caught nothing.

But notice this – even though Peter didn't think anything would happen, he decided to obey Christ's command. "Nevertheless," the tired, discouraged fisherman replied, "at Thy word I will let down the net." (Luke 5:5).

Now I wouldn't say that Peter was exactly strong in faith at that moment, would you? But what happened when Peter obeyed what Jesus told him to do? His net enclosed such a multitude of fish that he had to yell for his partners to come help him, and it took two boats to get the catch to shore!

Here's the lesson: If we wait until we are absolutely certain that God will hear us and answer our requests before we pray, we won't be doing much praying. Little question marks of doubt will always attempt to punctuate our thoughts. Therefore, even though we doubt we must obey His Word. We must do what He tells us to do:

"Ask," "Seek," "Knock,"

"Diligently seek Him"

"Pray without ceasing,"

"Let your requests be made known unto God,"

"Draw nigh to God," and so forth.

There is no doubt about it. *We have been commanded to pray.* When we do our part, He will do His.

Peter's faith was not perfect when his aching arms lowered that heavy, water-soaked net once more; he doubted that anything would happen. But he had enough faith to be obedient, and that's exactly how much faith it took to move the hand of God in his situation.

Now what does this have to do with you and your situation? Even though you're tired of trying, even though you have doubts, if you have enough faith to be *obedient* then you have enough faith for God to work through you. **If you have enough faith to obey, you have enough faith to move the hand of God.**

That is power principle number one. Put it into practice. And if you are approached by that reporter from the NBC Nightly News, just look into the camera and say with a confident smile, "I don't just believe that God answers prayer; I believe He will answer *my* prayer because I know that I have enough faith to move the hand of God!"

# Chapter Two
# Faith to Pray

In the first chapter we saw Peter and his partners, who had fished all night and caught nothing, rewarded with a huge catch of fish because this weary fisherman – even though he doubted – dared to obey Christ's command to launch out into the deep and let down his nets for a catch. In that account, we discovered power principle number one: *If you have enough faith to obey, you have enough faith to move the hand of God.*

For a second power principle, let's look at Acts 12:1-17. The writer informs us that the Roman emperor Herod had arrested James, the brother of John, and killed him with a sword. (We know from history that Herod Agrippa was a grandson of Herod the Great who ruled at the birth of Jesus, and that he was a zealous practicer of Jewish rites and a religious patriot). James was the first of twelve apostles to be martyred. The writer tells us when Herod saw the death of James pleased the Jews, he arrested Peter, also, put him in jail, and intended to kill him after the Passover. But the Scripture records that "prayer was made without ceasing of the church unto God, for him" (Acts 12:5).

I'd like to insert an observation here. The Bible doesn't say anything about prayer being made for James when he was in jail. We don't know if the church prayed or not. It is quite possible that they simply presumed that God would deliver James since Peter and John, with very little effort, were released from jail after the healing of the lame man at the gate of the temple (Acts 3:21). On another occasion, Peter and the other apostles were divinely delivered from prison during the night when an angel of the Lord opened the prison gates and led them out (Acts 5:12-19).

There doesn't seem to have been much labor in prayer in either of these instances; God just did it. Perhaps these believers had reached the point where they assumed they were invincible whether they prayed or not. I don't know that for a fact; however, I do know that you and I can presume upon the mercy and faithfulness of the Lord.

Today a lot of what some people call "faith" is actually nothing more than presumption. Often they have not revelation from God, no <u>Rhema</u> Word from the Lord for that particular situation. They just have the naïve attitude, "What will be will be. God is a good God. I don't need to put forth any effort in prayer. He knows what I need. It's going to turn out all right."

Now, I ask you, if that is the case, why did Jesus teach us to pray, "Lead us not into temptation, but deliver us from evil" (Matthew 6:13)? Why did the Son of God spend untold hours in prayer during His earthly ministry? Why did Christ warn His disciples, "Watch and pray lest ye enter into temptation? (Matthew 26:41)? If our prayers don't make any difference anyway, why pray?

I don't know whether the prayerless presumption of the early church contributed to the death of James or not. I do know that when Peter was thrown in jail, the church took action and prayed fervently without ceasing for him (Acts 12:5,12).

But were those saints in the early church praying with great faith? Were they absolutely positive that God would release Peter from prison? I'd like to say yes, but the scriptural account leads us to believe that the answer is no. After Peter realized an angel had rescued him from prison, he hurried to John Mark's house where many believers were praying. However, when he knocked at the door of the gate, and a servant girl ran in and announced that Peter was outside, the believers didn't believe her. As a matter of fact, they told the girl that she was crazy and that it wasn't Peter at all: It was either his angel or his ghost!

I'm sorry, but that doesn't sound like great faith to me! Those Christians didn't know for sure that Peter would be delivered; in fact, they were astonished when he appeared. But we shouldn't be too hard on them.

God doesn't always answer our prayers the way we thought He would, does He?

I think we can say with certainty that those early Christians praying so fervently for Peter's release were not praying with perfect faith. They didn't even know if their prayers would make a difference, but they had enough faith to pray. That's what mattered.

If you have enough faith to *obey* as Peter did when Jesus commanded him to launch out into the deep and let down his nets for a huge catch of fish, if you have enough faith to *pray* as the early church did in this situation (even though they didn't know how it was going to turn out), then you have enough faith for God to move through and accomplish what He longs to do.

Someone may be thinking, "Well, I believe Peter would have been delivered whether they prayed or not." Do you want to know what I think? I think Peter would have been killed if that angel hadn't delivered him from prison. And I believe the prayers of the saints determined what happened, not because they prayed with perfect faith, but because they had enough faith, imperfect as it was, for God to work through. They didn't know for sure what God *would* do, but they knew for sure what God *could* do. So, they prayed. And because they prayed, God was enabled to do what He wanted to do on behalf of Simon Peter. I don't know about you, but that makes me want to pray!

Your faith may not be perfect, but ***if you have enough faith to pray, then you have enough faith to move the hand of God.*** It is important that you understand that, because when you do, you won't let anything stop you from praying. You will develop a consistent prayer life, and prayer will become a vial necessity.

How much faith does it take to move the hand of God? It takes enough faith to obey as Peter, a tired, doubting fisherman, did. And, it takes enough faith to *pray* as the fearful but fervent early church did.

Next, we will look at the third of the four power principles in our study. It may be just the key you need to unlock your prayer life.

# Chapter Three

# Faith to Stay Persistent When God is Silent

Have you ever prayed as earnestly and sincerely as you knew how, and yet did not hear anything from God? If so, then you know that God's silence is one of the greatest tests of faith.

The Syrophoenician woman with the demon-possessed daughter experienced the Lord's silence. What was her response? Since Matthew was an eyewitness to the events that transpired that day, let's allow him to describe what happened:

> *Then Jesus went thence, and departed into the coasts of Tyre and Sidon.*
>
> *And, behold, a woman of Canaan came out of the same coasts, and cried unto him, saying, "Have mercy on me, O Lord, thou son of David; my daughter is grievously vexed with a devil."*

*But He answered her not a word. And his disciples came and besought him, saying, "Send her away; for she crieth after us." (Matthew 15:21-23).*

Even though this distressed woman was a Gentile, and did not have the Word of God in the measure that the Jewish people had it, she knew exactly what her daughter's problem was. She also knew who Jesus was, and that He had the power to cast out devils. But when she came to Jesus and begged of His help, He answered her not a word. He didn't acknowledge her presence or look in her direction.

What do you do when you pray and don't get an immediate answer? Do you keep on praying, or do you shrug and say, "Well, I guess the Lord just doesn't want to answer me?"

Notice this woman's attitude. She refused to give up and go home without her answer. Jesus was her daughter's only hope, and she knew it. The situation was desperate, *and so was she.* Therefore, pride and self-esteem were of no importance. Her daughter's healing was the only thing that mattered. And so, when Jesus refused to answer her cry for help, the desperate woman besought the aid of the disciples with loud, noisy, inarticulate, persistent cries.

What did the disciples do? The woman's crying embarrassed and annoyed the disciples, so they came to Jesus and begged Him to send her away. (I've always liked those men. They were such a compassionate group! If the Lord could do anything with *those* twelve guys, He can do something with *anybody!*) The disciples complained, "Lord, can't you do something with this woman? She keeps crying and making a big disturbance. Get rid of her, please."

Jesus had refused to help her. The disciples hadn't helped her. As a matter of fact, they were trying to get rid of her. Now, as if that were not enough, right in the woman's hearing, Jesus firmly declared, "I am not sent but unto the lost sheep of the house of Israel," (Matthew 15:24).

What was the woman's response when, for the second time, Jesus refused to help her? She fell at His feet, worshipped Him, and begged earnestly, "Lord, help me." Matthew records what happened next:

> *But He answered and said, "It is not meet to take the children's bread, and cast it to dogs.*
>
> *And she said, Truth, Lord: yet the dogs eat of the crumbs which fall from their masters' table, (Matthew 15:26,27)*

Can you believe He said that? Children (the lost sheep of the house of Israel) must be fed before dogs! What a comforting, encouraging, uplifting word *that* was! Most people would have stalked away with bitter angry tears trickling into their souls to water seeds of self-pity, roots of bitterness, and weeds of despair.

But this desperate woman had heard what wonderful miracles Jesus could do and what dynamic power He possessed. She knew He was her only hope. Therefore, she humbled herself even lower before the Lord. She pressed into His presence, flung herself upon His mercy, and replied tearfully, "Lord, I know what Jews think of people like me. I know my social position. I'm just an unworthy, helpless dog. But I'm not asking for the children's bread, Lord. Just give me a crumb from the table."

The compassionate heart of Jesus could stand it no longer. He turned, and His gentle eyes riveted upon her tear-stained, frantic face. "O woman," He marveled, "great is thy faith." And His next words were what the broken, desperate mother had longed to hear: "Be it unto thee even as thou wilt." Matthew concludes simply, "And her daughter was made whole from that very hour," (Matthew 15:28).

Now what does that heart-wrenching story say to you and me? First of all, we discover that Jesus sometimes delays an answer to prayer in order that our innermost attitudes might be revealed – to ourselves and to others – and in order to test and perfect our faith. We also learn that God's silence is not necessarily a denial. The fact that He does not answer us immediately does not mean that He will *not* answer or that He does not *want* to answer.

Zephaniah 3:17 contains an important kernel of truth: "...He will rest in His love..." That verse can also be translated, "...He will be *silent* in His love..." In His omniscient wisdom, God sometimes *loves us in silence.* Therefore, we must learn to press through the silence, for Jesus Himself promised:

> *"...Ask and keep on asking, and it shall be given you; seek and keep on seeking, and you shall find; knock and keep on knocking, and the door shall be opened to you.*
>
> *For everyone who asks and keeps on asking receives, and he who seeks and keeps on seeking finds, and to him who knocks and keeps on knocking the door shall be opened,"* (Luke 11:9,10 Amplified).

The Lord's first answer to us is not necessarily His final word. Therefore, if His answer to our prayers is not in keeping with His character and His promises, then we must be shamelessly persistent. That's the kind of faith Jesus commends and rewards.

The Syrophoenician woman's faith was not perfect. But the woman's persistence and humility won healing for her daughter. That is power principle number three: ***If you have enough faith to be persistent in prayer, then you have enough faith to move the hand of God.*** Say it with me: "I can move the hand of God." Now believe it. Act upon it. Refuse to be offended or discouraged by the Lord's silence. Press into His presence. Be persistent. Be humble. That's the kind of faith that moves the hand of God.

# Chapter Four
# Faith to Walk on Your Doubts

Let's pause for a moment and review what we have learned thus far in our study. You'll remember that first we looked at Simon Peter who dared to obey Christ's command to launch out into the deep and lower his net even though the weary fisherman and his partners had just completed a long night of fishing and had caught nothing (Luke 5:1-7). In that story, we discovered power principle number one: *If you have enough faith to obey, you have enough faith to move the hand of God.*

Next we studied the account of Peter's imprisonment and miraculous release due to the fervent prayers of the early church, even though they prayed with imperfect faith. In Acts chapter twelve, we saw those praying Christians shocked out of their wits when God answered their prayers we discovered power principle number two: *If you have enough faith to pray, you have enough faith to move the hand of God.*

For power principle number three, we turned to the moving story of the desperate Syrophoenician woman who refused to cease interceding for her demon-possessed daughter's deliverance, even though Jesus ignored her first pitiful cries for help (Matthew 15:21-18). We say a woman's persistence and humility win healing for her daughter, and through her example, a third power principle was revealed: ***If you have enough faith to be persistent in prayer, you have enough faith to move the hand of God.***

We have learned from the Scripture itself that **if we obey, pray, and persist, we can move the hand of God.** But I want to pose a question. Can doubt keep us from receiving, even after we have done all those things? Can doubt keep us from all the blessings and plans that God has in His heart for us? Matthew 14:22-32 is a good place to look for the answer to that perplexing question.

The disciples, you remember, were in a ship out in the middle of the Sea of Galilee. It was somewhere between three to six a.m., and their boat was being battered by raging waves and buffeted by contrary winds. As they peered through the darkness, suddenly their eyes riveted upon a ghostly figure tripping across the white-capped waves as if they were marble paving stones. Their fear and dread turned into amazement and relief as a familiar voice penetrated the darkness: 'Be of good cheer; it is I; be not afraid."

We all are acquainted with the surprising turn of events that followed. Peter, *at the Lord's invitation,* stepped over the side of the ship and walked right out across the waves toward Jesus. What do you think was going on the in the minds of the disciples as they stared incredulously at their impulsive comrade striding across the water? Personally, I don't think anybody in the boat was saying, "Come on, Peter!" Praise, God! You can make it, Buddy!" Unfortunately, that's not human nature. Human nature says, "That stupid guy. He won't make it. Who does he think he is, anyway? He's going down, sure as the world. He's going go under; you just hide and watch!"

If you don't believe me, try it and see. Get a word from the Lord and launch out in faith. Start a building project. Set a goal. Share your vision. Claim your healing. Step out on the water! The critics and prophets of doom won't cheer you on: instead, they'll sit in the safety of the boat with their arms folded, waiting for you to go under.

Remember: Peter was all pumped up and motivated because the Lord had said, "Come." Have you ever been way out on the water before you came to your senses and said to yourself, "Men don't walk on water! What in the world do I think I'm doing?" Here you were far away from the security of the boat, and not yet to where Jesus was, and you suddenly saw the ridiculously impossible situation your steps of faith had put you in. At that moment, ever so slowly, you began to sink. You weren't on top of things anymore; as a matter of fact, every step you took, you were getting in deeper. When you were almost in over your head did you do what Peter did and utter a frantic cry, "Lord, save me!"?

Notice what the Lord did and what He said. First, Jesus reached out and caught Peter. Then, He held Peter in His safe, sure grip and steered him back toward the boat, the Lord gently rebuked the drenched disciple: "O thou of little faith, wherefore didst thou doubt?"

Now, it's important that you get this. Jesus was not standing there with His arms crossed, tapping His foot, watching the doubting disciple disappearing under the rolling waves. Jesus wasn't delivering some lecture in a detached tone of voice: "You doubted, Peter. That's why you're going under. You'll probably drown. You've got doubt in your heart, and doubt won't float, you know. Sorry, I can't do anything for you. Too bad, Fella. I had big plans for you."

Dear, Lord! What kind of teaching is that? That's where we all live. Every one of us has been out on the water with doubt and faith struggling side by side in our hearts. Be honest. Isn't that the way it really is? Notice that Peter couldn't explain his doubts to Jesus, and neither can you. How can we explain to the omniscient, omnipotent, all-sufficient Creator God why we doubted His love, power, wisdom and goodness?

## To Move the Hand of God?

Let me show you something. The main difference between a Christian who walks in victory and a Christian who walks in defeat is just one thing. One allows his *doubts* to dominate his *faith,* and the other allows his *faith* to dominate his *doubts.* It's important that you grasp this. If you let doubt dominate your life, you won't be obedient, you won't pray, you won't be persistent. You will not be doing the kind of things that God can operate through.

It's not a matter of being free from all doubt. You'll have to deal with doubt as long as you live. It's a matter of walking on your doubts instead of walking in defeat. People say, "Oh, that Pastor Willhite. He's such an intercessor. He doesn't have any doubts." Do you know why I pray all the time? I pray because I refuse to be dominated by my doubts. Sure, I've seen great answers to prayer – but not because I had great faith. I simply obeyed, prayed, and persisted.

I don't listen to my doubts. Instead, I confess the things on earth that God has already said in heaven. Any when I do, the Lord says, "That's good enough, Son. I can work through that." God can work through you, right where you are, if you will not allow doubts to dominate your life, if you will not let fear keep you from praying and being persistent.

If you don't believe me, search the Scriptures and see if you can find a human being with absolutely perfect faith. Personally, I haven't found one. But I have found believers who just kept doing what the Lord told them to do. They prayed and persisted (even though their faith was imperfect), and they moved the hand of God. That's it!

**If you have enough faith to obey, pray, persist, and overcome your doubts, then you have enough faith to move the hand of God in your situation.** Nobody can stop you except yourself. You are the only one who can block what God wants to do in your life. Believe it!

Yes, you've heard me correctly. *Your* prayers can make a difference. Now let's get up, and get busy, my friend. We've got a lot of catching up to do!

# SECTION TWO
# THE MANUSCRIPTS
(Manuscripts produced from Pastor Willhite teaching the principles of prayer in conferences.)

# MORNING PRAYER CONFERENCE

*Manuscript 1*

# Introduction

The Lord has been giving me over quite a long number of years some truths that have made a real difference in my prayer life. I felt some time ago that I needed to share these things with people all across this country. The message that I want to bring to you is a message that I believe may be the most important thing that I've ever said on the subject of prayer.

Most people have the idea and believe that prayer does make a difference. They believe God answers prayer. They just have problem believing that God will hear their prayer. They are just not sure. They can imagine that God will hear someone like brother Oral Roberts or someone like Billy Graham or some famous person or some prophet or some priest. But they have a hard time believing that God would hear just little old me because I'm nobody, my faith is not very strong, and I really don't know if my prayers are strong enough to move the hand of God.

Well, the message that you're going to hear is a message that I believe will convince you once and for all that *your faith is strong enough to move the hand of God.* It may be weak, but it's strong enough. If you'll use it properly, it's strong enough to do or to accomplish the thing that God wants to accomplish. So, listen carefully to this word and let the Holy Spirit seal it in your spirit, and I believe you'll pray more effectively than you've ever prayed before in all of your life.

## Pleasing God

I want to share with you today from Hebrews chapter 11 and verse 6. Most of you can quote this scripture. It says, but without faith, it is impossible to please him, for he that comes to God must believe that he is and that he is a rewarder of them that diligently seek him.

Without faith it is not possible to please God. That's what the Word says here. Without faith it is not possible to please God, for they that come to God must believe that He is and that He is a rewarder of them that diligently, that faithfully, that persistently seek Him. That's what it means to be diligent. It means to keep doing it, to keep praying, to keep believing, to keep trusting in God.

He says that if we diligently seek Him, and I think we can prove this in the word of God, that diligent seeking of God is the greatest expression of faith. If I really do have faith, I will diligently seek Him, and if I do not have faith in my heart, then I cannot make myself diligently seek the Lord. It just doesn't happen. It just won't work. I just can't force myself into it. My diligent seeking of God will be an expression of my faith.

Now, by this scripture, all of us know that we have to have faith if we're going to really touch God or move the hand of God. The problem we have is we just don't know how much faith it takes. We're just not sure if we have quite enough and we hear a lot of faith teaching. Well, the teaching I'm about to share with you is a teaching, I promise you, you've never heard before. You've never read anything before like this, in any book. Any book that I've ever read on faith, doesn't say anything like what I'm going to say to you this morning.

Yes, it takes faith to move the hand of God, but how much faith does it take? Most people say, "Well, I know it takes faith and I believe it takes probably just a little more than I have. I don't know how much it takes, but I've got a feeling that it takes just a little bit more than I have. It just takes a little more faith than I've ever had in my heart."

Well, I'm going to show you that you have enough faith. You have enough faith to move the hand of God. Now you can see if you'll just think a little bit, that if you are questioning whether your faith is strong enough to move the hand of God, it'll be very difficult for you to be diligent in prayer. You'll always think, yes, God answers prayer. And I could ask the question this morning, how many of you believe that God answers prayer? And, of course in this place at 5 o'clock in the morning, everybody would say that, yes, I believe God answers prayer. So, we all believe that. It's just we are not really sure if He's going to answer my prayer. I just don't know if He's going to hear me. I know it takes faith and I'm not sure I have quite enough.

Well, you do have, and I'm going to show you by the scripture that you have enough faith to move the hand of God. When you get to where you believe that, you will diligently pray because you'll see that God hears you. Most of us believe that God hears Oral Roberts and great men of faith and power. We know he hears Kenneth Hagin and Kenneth Copeland and these great men of faith that teach on faith all the time. We're just sure that God hears them. But many times when we hear teaching on faith, it seems like it's presented in such a way that it's just a little bit beyond where I am. They said faith comes by hearing and I've been in church a lot and I've heard a lot of sermons, but it seems like my faith is still just a little inadequate, even though it's more than it used to be. It's a little stronger than it was, but it still seems to be just a little bit inadequate and not quite sufficient to really move the hand of God.

# Different Kinds of Faith

When I went through the scriptures and began to think about this and began to study about faith, I saw a lot of different kinds of faith presented and different measures of faith. The scripture says Roman chapter 12, verse 3, *that God has given to every man, the measure of faith.* That seems to indicate that maybe all of us have just about the same amount if we're Christians, because whatever we have is what God has given to us. So, maybe we have about the same amount. It could be that the difference between Christians is not the amount of faith they have, but what they do with what faith they have; how that faith is expressed; and how they give expression to that measure of faith that God has given them.

As I went through the scriptures, I found these kinds of words. I found that there was weak faith. So I can see a difference in quality of faith. I see that there's weak faith. I see there's great faith. I see there's little faith. I see much faith. I see this expression, no faith. I hear the disciples praying increase our faith. Of some Jesus said they were full of faith. One time Jesus said he saw their faith. I hear the apostles talking about people who are steadfast in faith, strong in faith, abounding in faith, established in faith, rich in faith. And I feel like I'm at that place where it says weak in faith most of the time.

I see all these different measures of faith and different qualities and quantities of faith, and where am I in all of this? Do I have enough faith to really move the hand of God? Am I just here wasting my time? This precious time that I gave up this morning to be in the house of God? Do I have enough faith to make any difference in God's plan of things? Do I have enough faith to really move the hand of God?

Well, I want to cite four examples in the scripture that I believe will help you to understand and know that you have enough faith and how to make the faith that you have operate in a positive, forceful way. I can show you how to do that.

Turn to Luke chapter 5. You'll see a story that you're very familiar with, but sometimes we just read it and just sort of look over it and don't really see what's being said. In this particular case, it says (beginning with verse 1), *It came to pass that as the people were pressed upon him to hear the word of God, he stood by the lake of Gennesaret and he saw two ships standing by the lake, but the fishermen were gone out of them and were washing their nets. And he entered into one of the ships, which was Simon's and prayed that he would thrust out a little from the land. And he sat down and taught the people out of the ship. And when he had left speaking, he said, under Simon launch out into the deep or launch out into the deep and let down your nets for a catch. And Simon answered him, said unto him, master, we have toiled all night and have taken nothing.*

"Now, Master, we are fishermen we've worked this lake, this Sea of Galilee. We've been here for years and we know how to fish. We know when the fish are running and when they're not running. We've been fishing all night. It's work to fish, Lord, and we are tired because we've been doing this all night long."

But then, even though all of these things I know were in his mind, (and I'll show you why I know that a little bit later on), but right here he said, he just simply said, "*Nevertheless, at thy word*, even though I don't believe anything's going to happen, even though I don't believe we're going to catch anything, nevertheless, at your word, I will let down the net. I will do what you're telling me to do. I don't think anything's going to happen." I'll tell you that right now. He didn't really say that. But in his heart, he was saying that. In his mind, he was saying that because that's what he really believed.

That's what his objection implied. When he said, "Lord, we have toiled all night and we have not caught anything. Nevertheless, at your word, I will let down the net." And so he launched out, he began to move. Didn't have much faith. Didn't have a lot of confidence.

Wasn't absolutely sure that they were going to catch anything.

Listen, if you're waiting to be absolutely certain that God's going to hear you in your time of prayer, then you probably won't ever pray, because there's always going to be some measure of doubt in you. It's going to be there. You're not going to always know for sure that what you pray is going to be heard and answered by God. You're just not going to always know that. Maybe sometimes you will, but there'll be a lot of times that you won't. If you're going to adjust your prayer life to whether or not you have freedom from doubt, then you won't be praying very much. I promise you that.

So, what happened here? Even though Peter was feeling all these things on the inside, he didn't express them right here. He was feeling them. He said, "Nevertheless Lord, regardless of what I feel about it, regardless of what I think might happen, I'm going to obey your word. I'm going to do what you're telling me to do. I'm going to do that."

And so, he just launched out and let down the nets for a catch and caught a great multitude of fish. In fact, more than he could get into his boat. He had to call his partners on the land and said, "Come and help us here. We've got more fish than we can get in the boat." And finally, when they got them all in and secured in the boat, look what happened to Peter.

When Peter saw it, he fell down at Jesus' feet saying, "Depart from me for I am a sinful man, Oh Lord." Why did he say such a thing as that? I really believe that what he was saying, "Lord, I didn't think we were going to catch anything. I didn't have any confidence at all that we were going to catch anything. And Lord, I'm such a doubter. Lord I'm just such a doubter. I didn't believe anything was going to happen. And look what's happened. We've got more fish than we know what to do with." He must have been thinking something like that, or he wouldn't have fallen down before the Lord and said, "Lord, just leave me. Just depart from me Lord. I'm not even worthy for you to be in my presence or for me to be in your presence."

## Faith Does Not Come by Seeing

How many of you ever felt that way sometimes? Peter had observed all the miracles that the Lord had done. He knew the kind of things that Jesus did, but you see *faith doesn't come by seeing things.* It doesn't come by seeing things. The people who had walked around and followed after Jesus all the time he was doing his miracles were the ones who were crying out, "Crucify him! Crucify him!" They'd come to doubt. All at once they were dominated by their doubts and they began to disbelieve rather than believe.

## Faith to Obey

Now I want to show you something here. *Peter's faith was not perfect* when he let down his nets for a catch of fish. He didn't think anything was going to happen, but **he had enough faith to be obedient** to the Lord's word. Now there's the key right there. Maybe you do not have a mind that is free from doubt, but if you've got enough faith to be obedient to the Lord, you have got enough faith for God to work through, to do what needs to be done in your life. Faith is not some mystical thing. *Faith is nothing more nor less than just simply <u>acting</u> upon the word of God*. It is acting upon what He said. And **if you've got enough faith to be obedient, you've got enough faith to move the hand of God.** Just enough to be obedient -that's all.

## The Feeling of Knowing

It doesn't require that feeling of just knowing. Oh, I just know! I just know it's going to happen, or I just have all the confidence in the world that this is going to come to pass, that it's going to be done just like this. Most of us don't enter into that realm very often. Sometimes we do, thank God, but most of the time we live in that place where doubt is always there. Even though faith is present, doubt is always there as well. And we are not really sure that God is going to do the thing that we want him to do. But if we have enough faith to be obedient to what God has said, we have enough faith to move Hs hand. We have enough faith to receive what God wants to do. So that's number one. *If you have enough faith to be obedient, you have enough faith to move the hand of God.*

## Faith to Pray

Let's look at Acts chapter 12. Most of you remember what was happening here in the history of the early church. The situation was such that Herod had arrested James and had killed him with the sword, and then, he also arrested Peter. His intent after the days of fasting and preparation for the Passover was to also kill Peter. That's what he intended to do. So, he had arrested him and was holding him in jail.

But the scripture says *that Peter therefore was kept in prison,* verse 5, *but prayer was made, but prayer was made without ceasing of the church under God for him.*

Now it doesn't say anything about prayer being made for James when he got in jail. It doesn't say whether the church prayed or not. I don't know if they did or not. It's quite possible that they just presumed that God would deliver James since Peter and John had been delivered from prison before that. There didn't seem to have been much effort in prayer and God had just done it. It may have been that the church had reached the point by that time that they just assumed they were invincible whether they prayed or not. It wouldn't make any difference. God would just always get them out of trouble.

# Presumption

Do you know that you can get to that place where you presume? I think a lot of things that people call faith is nothing less than presumption. They just presume that it's going to be a certain way. They have no revelation from God, no word from the Lord, and so they just go on just like everything's going to happen. Whatever is to be, is going to be, and we don't need to put forth any kind of an effort in prayer at all. But when James got killed with a sword, I know one thing, the church took action at that point in time. Maybe they were convicted by their prayerlessness concerning or in behalf of James, but it says, *but prayer was made without ceasing by the church unto God for him.*

They gathered at John Mark's house and were praying day and night. I don't know how many days had passed. I know Peter had been arrested during the days of unleavened bread, which were seven days prior to the Passover. So sometime during those seven days, he had been arrested and I know that it was the intent of Herod to kill him after the feast. In that seven day period there, after he'd been arrested the church had been praying. As soon as they knew he was in prison, they began to seek God. They began to pray as they gathered at John Mark's house. It said *they prayed without ceasing.* That meant they were praying day and night.

But let's see if they really believed anything was going to happen for sure. Were they were absolutely positive that something was going to happen and that he was going to be released from prison?

I think this story indicates that they were not really positive of that at all. When God did deliver him miraculously, he made his way directly to John Mark's house and started knocking on the gate (He knew a prayer meeting was going on there. I'm sure they'd got that word to him even while he was in prison).

Rhoda, the little servant girl, came and saw that it was Peter out there and ran back to the prayer meeting and said, "Peter's at the gate." They said, "It couldn't be. That's his spirit. It must be his spirit. They have probably killed him and his spirit has made an appearance out there at the gate." But when he kept knocking on the gate, they finally went and discovered that it really was Peter. He was delivered.

Now they weren't praying with perfect faith. They didn't know for sure if it was going to matter, but they had enough faith to pray. They weren't sure, they didn't know for sure, but they did have enough faith to pray. If you've got enough faith to obey like Peter did after he fished all night; if you've got enough faith to pray like this church prayed - They were sincere. They were devoted. They were seeking God day and night. It was faith that took them there to prayer, but it was not enough faith to cause them to just know that he was going to be delivered, when he was going to be delivered, or even that he was going to be delivered -but they kept praying just the same.

So, ***if you've got enough faith to obey*** what the Lord tells you to do, and you've got ***enough faith to pray and stay <u>persistent</u>,*** even though you may not know for sure if anything's going to happen, ***then you've got enough faith*** for God to move through to accomplish what He wants to accomplish.

Now somebody says, "Well, I think Peter would have been delivered, whether they prayed or not, don't you?"

You know what I'll say? *Absolutely not.* He would have been killed without doubt. As far as I'm concerned, if that angel had not delivered him from prison, he would have been killed. The church determined what happened. Not because their faith was perfect, but because they had enough faith for God to work through. He will not impose His good will on people either, but this people knew that God *could* do things like that. They knew that God *had done* things like that. And even though they were not sure that he was going to release Peter on this occasion, they prayed and God was enabled because of that. Because of what little faith they had, God was able to do what He wanted to do on behalf of Simon Peter on this occasion.

What keeps me wanting to pray? That just keeps me wanting to pray. No, my faith isn't perfect. I can certainly admit that and if I was trying to say it was, I'd be lying and that'd be bad. That's not just a positive confession. It's a lie. When I know that my faith is not perfect, but I'll tell you what it is. I've got enough. I've got enough faith to obey and I've got enough faith to pray. I've seen some miracles happen when I didn't think anything was going to happen. When I didn't have any personal faith that it was going to take place at all, I saw miracles come to pass because I prayed.

I'm telling you your prayers make a difference. Your prayers make a difference. What you do will make the difference in whether God is able to do what He wants to do or whether He doesn't do that. This is important for you to understand. If you don't, you'll never develop a consistent prayer life until you understand **that you've got enough faith to move the hand of God.** You've got enough faith to do it. You yourself have that much faith. If you've got *enough to obey*, if you've got *enough to pray*, you've got enough for God to work through, to accomplish what He wants to accomplish.

## Faith to Stay Persistent

But let's take another example: Let's look at Matthew chapter 15. Here you have the story of the Canaanite woman because of her persistent kind of appeal to the Lord. In verse 21 of chapter 15 of Matthew, *Then Jesus went thence and departed into the coast of Tyra and behold a woman of Canaan came out of the same coast and cried unto him saying, "Have mercy on me, Oh Lord thou son of David. My daughter is previously vexed with a devil."*

She knew what the problem was even though she did not have many of the advantages that the Jewish people had. She didn't have the word of God in the measure that the Jewish people had, but she did know who Jesus was. She knew that He was the son of David. She knew that He *could,* that He had the power to cast out devil. She knew that, and so she came praying to Him, *Lord Jesus thou son of David have mercy on me. My daughter is previously vexed with a devil* and look what it says in verse 23: *He answered her not a word.* He didn't even acknowledge her presence. He didn't even look in her direction. *He answered her, not a word*, not one word.

Now there's where the real test of faith comes. When you pray as earnestly and sincerely as you know how to pray, and you don't hear anything. How many has ever been there? You were praying, but you didn't get an answer. You didn't hear a word, not a thing. What do you do then? Do you keep on praying or do you say, "Well, I guess the Lord just isn't going to hear me."

Well, she just kept pressing her claim. Even when He *answered her not a word* and didn't say a thing to her, after she had pressed that claim again and again. It says His disciples came to Him and besought Him.

I always like these disciples. They're such a compassionate group of men, just have such love. Listen, if the Lord can do anything with those twelve, He can do something with anybody. That's the most motley group of people I've ever seen or ever read about in my life here.

Here this woman is. She's humbled herself before the Lord. She's crying out. *Lord, have mercy on me.* And they're saying, "Lord, do something about this. She's bothering us. She's crying here. She's just making a big. Well, she's just disturbing everything around here. So Lord, could you do something for her? Get rid of her some way for she's crying after us." And He said to them, not her. She hears it. She's there in their presence. He's still not talking, not answering, not saying a word to her, but to them, He says, *I'm not sent, but to the lost sheep of the house of Israel.*

People can't even take it if they don't hear something quickly. They're saying Lord, give me patience and do it right now. I've got to have it quickly."

But she had pressed into His presence and she had cried unto him. He *had not answered her a word.* He was talking to His disciples about her as though she was not even there in His presence. She falls down and worships Him, crying out, *Lord help me.* And He says, *I can't take the children's bread and cast it to dogs.* She said, "Lord, I'm a dog. I know that. I know what my position is. I know that I'm not worthy of these things, but Lord, even dogs can feed from the crumbs that fall from their master's table. And Lord, I'm just asking for a crumb."

And Jesus said, *Oh woman, great is thy faith. Be it unto thee, even as thou will.*

Now, what is He talking about? What is there in what this woman did that indicates she had great faith? She didn't really know what was going to happen for sure. She was pressing her claim. But Jesus said, *You have great faith*, and it seems to me what He was saying is: *The reason I know you have great faith is because of your persistence.* I know you have great faith because you won't take no for an answer. He gave her an answer. First of all, he gave her silence and she pressed on through that.

## Silence is Not Necessarily a Denial

You're going to have to press through silence or you'll never get anything from God. You're going to have to go through that because your faith is going to be tested. Many times the test of your faith is that God doesn't answer a word, that the Lord doesn't answer you. You're going to have to be persistent enough and tenacious enough and knowing that this is the kind of thing that the Lord does. You're going to have to press on through God's silence, because *silence is not necessarily a denial*. Just because God doesn't answer you immediately does not mean that He doesn't want to answer you or that He will not answer you.

She kept pressing through, and finally, He did say, *It's not right to take the children's bread and cast it to dogs*. When she finally got that word, that wasn't the answer she wanted and she pressed right on through.

I can say this without any hesitation that sometimes the Lord's first answer certainly is not His final word in the matter. She just kept right on. That first answer, that first word that He gave her was not the word that she was looking for. It was not the thing she desired. It was not what she knew she could have or she felt like she could have, if she could just press along through it. So, she just kept pressing her claim.

I'm here to tell you that ***if you've got <u>enough faith to be obedient</u>, if you've got <u>enough faith to pray</u> and you've got <u>enough faith to be persistent</u>, you've got enough faith to move the hand of God.***

Now who cannot be obedient? Anyone that just can't be obedient to what God's telling you to do? No, we can all do that. Is there anyone that cannot pray? No, we can all do that. Is there anyone that cannot be persistent? That's not too difficult. That's not beyond the scope of what I'm able to do. I can be persistent. I can be obedient. I can pray and I can be persistent. *And anyone who has enough faith to obey, enough faith to pray and enough faith to be persistent -*anyone who knows the Lord and knows what kind of things the Lord does and has some little understanding of the will of God, *that person can move the hand of God.*

I want us to say it together:

*I can move the hand of God.*

(Response) *I can move the hand of God.*

*I can do it.*

(Response) *I can do it.*

*I can obey.*

*(Response) I can obey.*

*I can pray.*

*(Response) I can pray.*

*I can be persistent.*

*(Response)I can be persistent.*

## What about Doubt?

But what about these doubts? What about these doubts that come into my mind? Pastor, I sometimes doubt. What about that? Am I going to be disqualified because I have all these doubts? Well, let's see if you will or not. Let's see if doubt disqualifies us. Let's see if our faith has to be perfect.

We know that if we're obedient, if we pray and if we persist, we see that those are the positive kind of things that move the hand of God. Can doubt keep us from receiving? Even after we've done all these things, can doubt keep us from receiving what God wants to do in our lives?

I think we've got probably the best and most clear, pure example and illustration of the fact that doubt and faith live side by side in all of us, in the example of the Apostle Peter. I like this man. I identify with him real well. I really do in many different ways, but especially on this occasion, in the 14th chapter of the gospel of Matthew.

In Matthew, chapter 14 verses 22 and 23, you'll see this record. Jesus had just fed a multitude of people and had ministered to them and had left some 10,000 of them to go up into the hills to pray. In fact, you see Jesus praying and then you see Him going through a day of ministry and then you see Him back in the place of prayer. So that every miracle that Jesus did, all of His ministry happened between the places of prayer that you see in His life.

**First prayer,**

**then ministry,**

**then prayer,**

**then ministry,**

**then prayer.**

You see it all the way through the life of Jesus. *Rising up a great while before day, He departs out into a solitary place.* He's praying. Leaving the multitude He goes up into the mountain to pray. You see Him spending all night in prayer. One prayer place to the next prayer place between those prayer places, the ministry of the Lord Jesus Christ. That's the way it ought to be for us. We ought to begin with prayer, minister, end with prayer, and begin with prayer, minister. And then again, right back through the cycle, because that's the only way we can have an effective ministry.

But here's Peter in this story in the 14th chapter. After Jesus had prayed all night, He'd sent His disciples on across. They were in the boat and the winds were contrary. They had not made very good progress and Jesus came to them the scripture says, *walking on the water*. He'd sent them on ahead of Him. The ship was now in the midst to the sea tossed with waves. *On the fourth watch, Jesus came walking on the sea, and when the disciples saw him walking on the sea, they were troubled saying, it is a spirit. And they cried out for fear and straight way Jesus spoke to them and said, be of good cheer, it is I. Be not afraid.* And Peter answered him and said, "Lord, if that's you out there, if that's really you out there bid me come to you on the water." And Jesus said, *Come.*

I like this story, and Peter, I mean, he just jumps out over the side of that boat. Here he goes. Just walking right out across the water. Right out there. Now, here's the boat over here. Here's Jesus over here, and he's out on the water. Now those guys sitting back in the boat, I know what was going through their minds. They said, "That stupid guy. He won't make it." That's what they were thinking. I don't believe there's anybody back there saying, "Praise God, go on Peter. You can make it." No, human nature is to say, if somebody does something out of the ordinary, "He's not going to make. He'll drown. He'll go under. You just watch and see."

You start a building project like we've got and you get out on the water. You're out there. I mean, out on the water, and everybody's waiting for the thing to go under - not everybody, but a lot of people. The critics are all there. Even some Christians, prophets of doom, are saying, "They won't make it. That's too big. Nobody can do that."

But here's Peter out on the water. He's all pumped up all at once, he was motivated. When the Lord said, *Come,* he was moved.

Listen, I've been moved sometimes. I mean I was out way out on the water before I came to myself and suddenly realized that men don't walk on water and here I was out there from the safety of the boat. I wasn't where Jesus was, yet I'm just out there.

The Bible said when he suddenly saw the situation and realized what had happened, where he was, that he began to sink. He began to go down. Now, I don't know how fast he was going down. Water doesn't just hold you up a little. I don't know whether he just started sinking. He just began to go down real slow. I think he did. I think that's what started happening. All at once he realized he was not on top of the water. He was nearly knee deep and every step he took he was getting deeper. He suddenly realized this is not working out the way I thought it was going to, and all at once he cries out, "Lord save me. "

## To Move the Hand of God?

And so, the Lord suddenly was there. Hallelujah. He didn't say, "You impulsive faithless person." He didn't say that to Peter. He didn't start giving him a lecture on the weakness of his faith at that point. It was after He got him back up on the top of the water, after they started going back toward the boat, He said, *Peter, why did you doubt?* He didn't say it while he was going down, *You've doubted, you doubted, Peter, that's why you're going under. You'll just probably drown.*

## Faith & Doubt Live Side by Side

Well, you've got doubt in you. I can't do anything for you. You've got doubt in your heart. Dear Lord, what kind of teaching is that? That's where we all live. Every one of us has been out there on the water, and I mean, it looked like our faith was working great. And all at once, we started sinking and we called unto the Lord. Our doubt was causing us to sink and our faith was causing us to cry out, "Lord save me." *Faith and doubt living side by side in every one of us all the time.*

I said you've never heard anything quite like this, but let's just be honest. Isn't that the way it really is? It's alright to be honest in God's house, isn't it? And everywhere else? Yes.

He said, *Peter, why did you doubt?* I've searched real carefully, and I do not find any attempted response on the part of this impulsive man. He didn't try to explain why he had doubted because no one can ever explain why they doubt. We don't have an explanation for that. I don't know why I'm walking along so well with absolute confidence, and all at once, I can't understand why, but doubt begins to come into my mind and I begin to be fearful.

*Why Peter*? Silence. Peter may have thought to himself, "I don't know why. I can't explain it Lord. I know I was doing good, but all at once, I don't know why, but I started..." He didn't even argue with the Lord about this at all. Didn't try to explain it. No need for us to try to explain it.

Now, let me show you something. The main difference between the Christian who walks in victory and the Christian who walks in defeat, the main difference is that they both have doubts. Both Christians have doubts. All Christians have doubts. I'll prove it. How many of you have ever had doubts in your mind and you're walking with the Lord?

We all do. So we're all facing the very same thing. The difference between the one who walks in victory and the one who is overcome by defeat is *the one who walks in victory is not dominated by his doubts*. He does not allow doubt to dominate his life because if doubt dominates your life, you know what will happen? You won't be obedient. You won't pray. You won't be persistent. If doubt is dominating your life, you won't be doing the kind of things that God can operate through. So it's not a matter of being free of all doubt.

***How much faith does it take
to move the hand of God?***

*Just enough to be obedient,*

*just enough to pray,*

*just enough to be persistent,*

<u>*just enough to overcome the doubts*</u>

<u>*that all of us have to deal with all of our life.*</u>

You'll never come to a time in your life when there will not be doubts going through your mind, because that's all the mind is capable of doing. It's capable of questioning everything that God does.

I remember when Ronnie Cohen came to our church years ago. He had gone through a healing line at 12 or 13 years old in Tulsa, Oklahoma. The lady evangelist said to him that he was coming for a chest cold or something like that. She noticed something was wrong with his left eye. She said, "Can you see out of that eye?" He said, "No, I can't see." She prayed and all at once he could see. She did not know that there was no eye there. It was just a plastic eye. He could see and read whatever she gave him to read. Of course the miracle hit the newspaper. The Tulsa World carried it the next day.

My uncle, who was blind, lived in Tulsa. The family saw the news print: *Boy sees through plastic eye.* He thought somebody had invented a new kind of mechanism for seeing. They read the story. He went to that meeting. A few years after that, Ron was traveling around giving this testimony and he came to our church. I'll tell you, the house was filled. Everybody in the community came, and sure enough, he would just read whatever you handed him with this other eye bandage up. Then he'd flip it out and read it with an empty socket - nothing there. Because of God, it was just a miracle - just one of those miracles that God did. Do you know what happened when people came down to see that? Those who believed said, "Praise the Lord, hallelujah." Those who doubted said, "I wonder how he does it. That must be some kind of trick."

Let me state this about your mind. If you are sad and bent in that direction, you're going to be doubtful. The doubts will come. Those doubt thoughts will come to your mind, but you cannot let them dominate your life or you'll walk in defeat every day. You won't pray. You won't believe God for anything.

I don't suppose anybody has more doubt thoughts than this preacher does and always have had. I've always had them all of my life. I know people say, "Pastor Willhite, he's such a prayer. He surely would never have any doubts. He prays all the time.

You know why I pray all the time? Because I refuse to be dominated by my doubts. I keep right on praying and I've seen great things happen. Not because I had faith, but because I persisted. Because I kept doing it because I believe that God does this kind of thing. I can't say that I always know that He's going to, but I pray. I know it's the kind of thing He does. I know it's the kind of thing that He says He will do. Although I may not be able to be totally free from doubt in my mind, I bring my body under subjection and I confess the things on earth that God has already said in heaven. And the Lord says, *That's good enough, son. That's all right. I can work through that. I can work with that.*

God can work with you, right where you are. If you will not let doubt dominate your life; if you will not allow those doubts and fears to dominate and to keep you from praying and to keep you from being persistent, you can receive the things that God has in store for your life.

Hallelujah. Now what I'm telling you is the truth about faith. It's the truth about it. I've went through the scripture since I began to see these things clearly, and I didn't find anybody in the word of God that was perfect in faith. Most of them were great big doubters. Hezekiah was given the message from no minor prophet, by the way. Isaiah said, *Set your house in order, you're going to die and you're not going to live.*

I mean this guy didn't miss it, really. He was a true prophet of God. Old Hezekiah turned his face to the wall and began to pray and began to seek God. He started crying out to God and weeping with tears, and before Isaiah got halfway across the city, the spirit of the Lord spoke to him again and said, *Go back to Hezekiah, and tell him I'm going to add 15 years to his life.*

I won't demonstrate this again, but I know that if Isaiah had been like most of us, we would not have wanted to give the second word, especially if it was absolutely contrary, diametrically opposed to the first word we gave. But he had a word from God, *You're going to die. You're not going to live.* But the scripture says, *God said, I heard his cry and I saw his tears. I've heard his cry. I've saw his tears. Now you go back and tell him he's going to live and not die.* Now isn't that a strange thing? He delivered the message and you know what? Hezekiah believed that he was going to die and not live, but he didn't believe he was going to live and not die.

He said, "Well, Isaiah, could you give me a sign of some kind? I need a little bit further proof of this. I got that first message and I believe that one, but this one here, I'm having trouble with."

Listen, go through the scriptures. You won't see any men of women of perfect faith. They're not there. They're just people who learned to overcome their doubts. They're not dominated by doubts. They just kept doing what the Lord told them to do. They just persisted. They just kept praying and believed. They kept praying sometimes not believing perfectly, but they kept praying.

The Bible says concerning those people who came to Jesus, bringing the paralyzed man and letting him down into His presence, *When Jesus saw their faith*, He ministered to the man. *When He saw their faith.* Faith is something you see. So if you've got enough faith to obey, enough faith to pray, enough faith to be persistent, enough faith to act, to do what you feel in your heart is going to be the thing God wants you to do - if you've got enough faith to do that, *then you've got enough faith to move the hand of God*. You have got enough faith to move the hand of God. Nobody can stop you, but yourself. You are the only one that can stop what God wants to do in your life.

## Concluding Remarks

Thank you for letting me share this message with you on what I believe to be one of the most important aspects of prayer, and I trust that God will just seal this into your spirit and you will come to realize, without any question at all, that if you have enough faith to obey, that's all it takes just enough faith to obey and just enough faith to be persistent. When you know, you're praying in the will of God, your prayers will move the hand of God. You **do** have enough faith. *You do have enough faith to move the hand of God.* If you have enough faith to obey, to pray, and you have enough faith to be persistent. You don't have to be free from doubt. You don't have to be free, completely free, from questioning at all, because we understood from the message that I just preached that many of the people of God, who certainly that did great things for God, had many doubts and sometimes many fears, but they were able to overcome those things. They were not dominated by their doubts. They overcame their doubts and pressed right on and received the very thing that they were asking God for.

# **Prayer**

*Father, I ask you now in the name of Jesus, take this word and cause it to be life in these precious ones, Lord, that you brought here for this time together. Let us never be dominated by our doubt, oh God, but let us determine right now that we will obey you when we hear your word. We will pray. We will persist. We will overcome because we can do, every one of us can do these things and we can do them faithfully. And as we do them, we know Lord that you will work through them to the accomplishment of your will in our generation. And thank you for that Lord. Hallelujah. Hallelujah.*

# NATIONAL CALL TO PRAYER CONFERENCE

*Manuscript 2*

## Dealing with Doubt

Hebrews 11: But without faith, it is impossible to please him. For he who comes to God must believe he is. And that he is a rewarder of those who diligently seek him.

This is called the faith chapter of the Bible because God is talking a lot about the different men of faith that did wonderful and mighty things through faith in God. God ministering and meeting their faith with answers.

Now in verse six, He says we understand that without faith, without faith, in some amount, without faith in some amount, it is impossible to please God. So, we know we have to have some amount of faith. It does not say how much faith is required to please God, it just says faith.

Because we're always thinking in human terms of some kind of measurement, you know, well now how much faith then? How much faith does it take to please God? Do I have enough faith to really please God? We think about that and wonder about that. A lot of us are come up with a conclusion that however much it may take, how much faith it may take to please God, I think it's just a little more than I have. I think that's the way we sort of view things. We feel like it takes some amount. We don't know exactly how much, but we think it's probably just a little bit more than we have.

Of course that doesn't help you and encourage you to pray if you start thinking that you know faith is required and you're not sure you have enough. Then you'll tend to sort of leave the praying up to the people who you feel may have faith. Their measure is a little bit higher than yours, and maybe they can pray effectively and you can't.

I want to tell you tonight that you can pray whatever amount of faith you have. Whether it's a little faith or a lot of faith, you have sufficient faith to please God. And if you do have sufficient faith to please God, then you can pray prayers that God will answer, because you do have faith. You have faith.

# The Test

I want to give you a test to prove that you have faith. There are only two or three questions here on the test, but the test is simply this. *They that come to God*, it says, *must believe He is*. So let me ask the first question. Do you believe God is? Do you believe, I'm talking about really, do you *really* believe God is?

Well, let's say it: *I believe God is.*

**Audience Response:** *I believe God is.*

Well there's just two questions, really. It says that we must believe God is, and *that He is a rewarder of those who diligently seek Him*. So the second question is, do you believe God is a rewarder of those who diligently seek him?

**Audience Response:** *Yes*

You really do. So you believe God is, number one. We all answered that. I think everybody said yes, I believe God is. And now I think everybody has said, I believe God is a rewarder of those who diligently see Him. Well, you've just passed the test. That's all that is required to pray effectively. You don't have to have any more faith than that to pray effectively. Now you may need some further understanding, but faith is not the problem. If you believe God is, and you believe He is a rewarder of those who diligently seek Him, then you have sufficient faith to please God and thus to receive answers to your prayers.

You ought to be a little bit happy about that, because you passed the test. You've got faith. So, it's not a faith problem that's keeping your prayers from being answered.

Listen, I want you to know that there is an enemy and his name is Satan and he doesn't want you to know that you have faith. He wants you to believe that you don't have sufficient faith to move the hand of God. That's what he's trying to convince us all, that we just don't have faith enough to get the answer that we're seeking for. It takes some amount of faith, but I think it's just a little bit more than I have.

I see some heads going like that. Yes. Yes. That's where I am. I know it takes faith and I don't think I have enough. Now I've just now shown you by the scripture that you have sufficient faith, because you've said I believe God is, and let's just put it even more simple. Let's just say, and I believe God can.

**Audience Response:** *I believe God can.*

I believe He is and I believe He can. He has the power and He does hear those who diligently seek Him. I know there are people who believe and teach that we must believe God will and that just believing He can is not enough. I'm not going to be critical of anyone because most of these people that might have that opinion probably have done more than I have ever done. But I am not of the opinion that you have to believe God will, you only have to believe God can, and then diligently pray that He will.

## The Leper

You remember that leper that came to the Lord and said, Lord, I know, I know if you will, you can make me whole. I don't know if you will, but I certainly know you can. And Jesus said, Well, that's good enough for me. Be healed, be whole.

No, you may not know. You may not have that revelation that God will, but you know He can. Then you determine in your heart, I'm going to pray that He will, and I'm going to keep on praying. I'm not going to stop praying. I'm going to pray diligently that the one who I know can, will do what I'm asking Him to do.

So, now we know that faith is required. We know that we have the amount of faith necessary to move the hand of God. And, because we believe God is, and we believe he is a rewarder of those that diligently seek him, we understand now that it doesn't mean that I could just ask God for everything or anything that comes into my mind. It's a matter of getting my will right in the center of His will, by being concerned about what He has told me to do and working at that very thing. My prayers are going to be focused on what it takes to get the work done that God has given me to do, because it's really about Him and about His kingdom.

It's not about us. The only reason I need strength is to do what He told me to do. The only reason I need money is to get the work done that He's told me to do. So, we've got the faith part of it fixed, but we have another problem. We also have doubt.

"Well," somebody is saying, "Well, I don't know if you can have faith and doubt at the same time." Of course you can. Everyone does. We have faith. We believe God is, we believe God can, but just as surely as we have faith, we also have doubt. Somebody who says they never doubt, better watch what they're saying. It might not be the truth, because we all doubt.

## Doubt is Learned

We weren't born with doubt. We weren't born with it. We were born trusting. We learned to doubt. We learned right away. As a child growing up, we learned right away that things are not always the way that we were told they were.

Our parents said that there were bunnies that lay eggs at Easter time, or there's a Santa Claus that comes down the chimney and brings gifts. Well, little children learn after a little while that that's not true. That's not true. So, they begin to question. Then when they go to public school, one of the first things that begins to happen is that they're taught not to believe anything that you can't prove in the scientific test tube of some kind. So don't believe any of what you hear, you've got to be able to prove it.

Doubt begins to creep in even where faith rests. Where faith is there's also doubt, but I'm thankful to God that I learned something about doubt. It's here. Faith is here. While I have faith in my heart, believing God is and God can; my head may be telling me, but it's not going to happen. Or my doubt may be telling me, it's not going to happen, because doubt is up here in my head.

## John the Baptist Doubt?

Now just to show you that you're in good company as a doubter, I want to show you that we have a lot of doubter characters in the New Testament. One of the great characters in the New Testament was a man by the name of John, the First Baptist. You remember that guy? He happened to be baptizing one day when his cousin, Jesus, appears and comes to him for water baptism.

John said, "Jesus, I need to be baptized of you. I'm the one that needs baptism. I need your baptism. You don't need my baptism." And Jesus said, *You suffer it to be so, this is the way it's supposed to be right now.* And so, John baptized Jesus in the Jordan river and when He came up out of the water, the Spirit descended upon Jesus in the form of a dove. God spoke out of heaven saying, *This is my beloved son in whom I am well pleased.*

What an experience! Has anyone ever had that kind an experience? Nobody? Probably not many, at least if maybe some have, but John heard. John saw. John heard. You would think there's no possible way he could ever question or doubt that revelation, but he did. In the 11th chapter of Matthew, verse one, if you'll read that story, you'll find that that John heard of the works of Jesus and what he heard so troubled him that he sent two of his disciples to inquire, "Are you really the one or should we look for another?"

Now what on earth would have disturbed John to the point he began to question the revelation he had received and what would've caused that? The only thing I could think of that would've caused him to have such doubt at that point in his life was I believe that he *heard* of the works of Jesus. And when he heard of the works of Jesus, he began to question the revelation that he had seen that he'd received.

That work, I believe that he heard about, was that Jesus had attended a wedding feast in Cana of Galilee. John wouldn't have been caught dead there because he was an antisocial. I mean, he stayed away from the people as much as possible. If they came to him, he would baptize them after questioning them to some extent. He would baptize them, but he was not going to go to a social event.

He *heard* that Jesus went there, and if that weren't enough, He had turned barrels of water into wine. John was a teetotaler, never had tasted it. And if this Jesus, his cousin here has not only attended this festival or this ceremony and this celebration, He had turned water into wine and a lot of it.

And so John says, this can't be the one because John fully expected that Jesus was going to be more austere than he was. He was going to be much more holy than he was. And yet Jesus, well I'm sure he heard about him eating with tax collectors and sinners and all of this, just didn't add up because you see John had unrealistic expectations. Many of us have struggles because we expect things that probably are not realistic in some cases.

But alright, he sends these disciples over to Jesus and they questioned Jesus. "Now John sent us here and he wants to know, are you really the one or should we look for another?" And Jesus said, *Go tell John, you go tell John that the blind see, that the deaf hear, that the cripples are walking. You go tell John of these miracles that you can see going on here.* And then He added a little parenthetical statement at the end, *And by the way,* He said, *Tell John, blessed is that person who does not, who is not offended in me.* Well, John was a doubter, a questioner.

## Peter, Why Did You Doubt?

If that weren't enough, here is Peter who became the first choice of the Lord to open the door to the people on the day of Pentecost to preach that great sermon recorded in the second chapter of Acts. Peter was a doubter. Yes, he was.

One night they were trying to get across the lake. Jesus had told them to go across the Sea of Galilee to the other side and wait for him there. They got in the boat and started across, but they were rowing against the contrary winds and they just weren't making a lot of headway. Then along about 4 o'clock in the morning, they looked out and could see a white clad figure out on the water. They assumed it was a ghost and got really scared until they heard the voice of Jesus or heard a voice say, *Don't be afraid, it's me.*

And Peter says, "Lord, if that's you out there bid me come to you on the water." And Jesus said, *Come.* Well, Peter just stepped over the side onto the water, and he begins to walk toward Jesus on the water. Those guys in the boat are saying, "There he is -a big show off again." I mean, they're hoping he'll sink. Because if he sinks, they're going to look so much the wiser for having stayed in the safety of the boat. You see? So they're hoping he's going to go down and it's not very long until he's up knee deep.

He realizes he's going down. Because he starts sinking, he starts thinking. See his mind kicked in and the doubt factor began to work. He's walking by faith and suddenly all at once this doubt kicks in and he starts to sink and then he cries out. His faith then checks back in. The doubt is taking him down and faith caused him to cry out, "Help me, Lord Jesus."

Suddenly, Jesus is there. He gets him by the hand, gets him stabilized, and they both together walk back toward the boat. As they're walking along, I think Jesus said with just the slight smile, *Why did you doubt? Why did you doubt?*

Now Peter isn't known for having nothing to say. In fact, on one occasion, it said having nothing to say, "he said," when he was in the Mount of Transfiguration.

But I don't find any place where he ever tried to answer that question. In fact, that's a question that's difficult to answer. You could be walking along so well. I mean, walking on water. I mean literally doing the impossible and everything is just going great. And suddenly, I mean just out of nowhere, suddenly doubt thoughts begin to fill your mind, and the first thing you know you're sinking. By faith you were walking, and all at once doubt begins to settle in and down you begin to go. Then faith kicks in, "Lord help me" and the Lord didn't say, "Drown you doubter you." No, He didn't do that. No, He took hold of him.

We doubt. Yes, we do. We don't doubt that God is. We don't doubt that God can. We doubt our faith. We doubt our worthiness. All kinds of things we can begin to doubt, and suddenly when we do, then things begin to sort of crumble.

So here, you've got John the Baptist and then you've got Peter before the day of Pentecost. I'm hearing somebody say, "Yes, but after they got full of the Holy Ghost, no more doubt." Well, if you believe that I've got some ocean front property in Arizona.

Anyway, after the day of Pentecost, well after they were filled with the Holy Spirit, 12th chapter of the book of Acts opens with these words, *Herod killed James with a sword*. Well, you don't think shock waves went through the spirit filled church in Jerusalem at that time? They fully expected that James to be set free. It also says in the next verse that Herod arrested Peter and had stated that he was going to do the same to Peter after the days of Unleavened Bread. The church didn't expect that. They expected he was going to be delivered. It had happened in the past.

# The Spirit Filled Church Doubt?

People had been delivered from prison and they fully expected it to happen again. I don't even think they prayed about it. I really don't believe they prayed. They just made a positive confession. Somebody says, "What do you think is going to happen to James?" "Oh, he'll be out in a few days. Don't worry about it. It's happened before. God's going to take care of him. He'll be out." Sure enough, he was, but he was dead. I mean, suddenly their faith was shaken to the core and they were filled with doubt, but they called a prayer meeting. Yes, they did and they began to pray 24 hours a day, round the clock. We don't know. It may have been a day or two or three. We don't know exactly how long that happened, but in a day or two, an angel came and led Peter right out of the prison. I mean, the doors just swung open.

Peter thought he was having a vision or a dream. He didn't know it was real until he got completely outside the prison. All at once he realized he was awake, that this is something that actually happened and he's out of prison now.

Peter knows about the prayer meeting because it says the church was praying at John Mark's house. Now, I don't know how big the church was at that time, but I know that John Mark's house wasn't big enough to handle 15,000 people. That was the estimated number of people who were in the church at that time. I don't think he had a house big enough to hold those. So, probably not of very many people showed up at the prayer meeting. Usually that's the case, not very many people and you can imagine why, because James had just been beheaded.

I mean, they thought he was going to be, their faith said, "He's going to be delivered." Their faith had laid hold of that, but it hadn't happened. They've just had James's funeral and now Peter's in prison and Herod has already said what he's going to do. But here's Peter, he's outside the prison. He heads down toward John Mark's house. He knocks on the outer enclosure of the compound at the gate.

Rhoda, a little servant girl, heard his knock and came to answer, to find out who it was, enquired, and heard the voice of Peter saying, "It's me." She forgot to unlatch the gate. She ran right back into the prayer meeting where she with bated breath announced, "Peter is out there at the gate. He's right out there at the gate."

Listen to their response, "Have you lost your mind?" That's what they said. "Are you mad? Are you crazy?" Another one said, "Oh, they've killed him. It's his spirit. He's just stopped by to say goodbyes and he goes to heaven."

Now they were praying day and night, but when the prayer was answered they couldn't believe it. Now I want to know how many people are honest enough to say you've had prayers answered, and you just said, "I can't believe it." I have, I guarantee you I've had prayers answered, and I just had to say, "Well, I just can't believe it."

Listen. Do you think they were praying with perfect faith? They knew God. They believe God was, that He is, and they knew that God could do it. They didn't know that He would, but they were praying nevertheless.

Is anybody getting anything out of this? Listen, it doesn't matter if you doubt. Pray. Just keep praying. It doesn't matter, because you also believe. You believe God is and you believe God can, and <u>you're not going to let the doubt that is in your head dominate the faith that is in your heart.</u>

So, I made up my mind a long time ago and I said it this way:

**I will not allow
the doubt that is in my head
to dominate the faith that is in my heart.**

*God is, and God can, and I'm going to pray that he will, until this issue is resolved one way or the other, a*nd it will be resolved. You will find God answering that prayer, even though you've confessed that you've got doubt in your head.

It's no hindrance, listen, doubt is no hindrance to prayer unless it keeps you from praying.

> ***If it keeps you from praying,
> then doubt has won the victory.***

So don't stop if there's doubt, don't stop praying. Just keep right on praying because in your heart you're saying, "I know God is, and I know God can, and I'm not going to stop praying or give up, I'm going to keep praying."

"Yes, but do you doubt?"

Sure. I doubt. I'm going to be truthful about it. Yes, I doubt, but doubt is not going to dominate the faith that is in my heart. That's a decision I have the power to make.

> ***I will not.
> I will not allow
> the doubt that is in my head
> to dominate the faith that is in my heart.***

> ***God is,
> and God can, and
> I'm going to pray that He
> will until this issue is resolved.***

# PASTORS CONFERENCE

## *Manuscript 3*

# Speaking To Pastors

The problem that most people have that have allowed their prayer life to degenerate to the point of praying only for the most part in emergency types of situations, is the result of coming to a kind of mindset that even though prayer is something that is important and that it is for many people an effectual thing, for them, it is not. They believe other people pray effectually, but they're not sure they pray effectually. And of course, if you don't know if your prayers are making any real difference, then you're going to leave most of the praying to people whose prayers you believe will make a difference. I've come to that place where I'm not sure that my prayers matter. I believe somebody's prayers matter, but I'm not sure mine do. You see?

## Spiritual Inferiority

Even when there is an answer to a prayer that I have prayed, I'm often of the mind to believe that it was probably somebody else's prayer that really touched God. Because our people, for the most part have a spiritual inferiority complex. That's the way it really is. People tend to feel that even though prayer is important and that God does answer prayer, they have a lot of difficulty really in their heart believing that God has heard my prayer. Because we know ourselves and we know how insignificant we are, and we know how limited our faith is. We know how much doubt is in our mind when we are praying. So even if there seems to be an answer, we are inclined to believe that the answer is the result of somebody else's prayer, not ours.

If we're going to have people praying consistently, we've got to cause them to believe that God does hear and respond to their prayer. They can pray effectually. For the Bible says in James chapter 5 verse 16, *the effectual fervent prayer of a righteous or a person in right standing with God has the potential to release tremendous power.*

The effectual fervent prayer of a person in right standing with God. Now for so many of us, even that little qualification that James makes here, discourages us. Satan is good at quoting scriptures, and when he quotes that scripture, he puts all the emphasis on a righteous person.

Since we don't feel righteous and we see a lot of inconsistencies in our lives, we understand that our lack of what we believe is a mountain moving faith. That's the only kind of faith that we hear people talking about today - mountain moving kind of faith, and we can't even move a mole hill. We are having difficulty believing that our faith is going to make any difference because we see that it's so insignificant. It's so limited, and the result is many people have just about given up praying other than when they just sort of have to. I mean, it's an emergency and they're going to cry out in desperation because that's the only thing I can do in this situation. I'll pray without knowing whether or not my prayer is going to make any significant difference.

## Your Prayers Make a Difference

Now what I want to help you to do as pastors, not only to know that your prayers make a difference, but I want to help you to be able to say things to the your people that will cause them to believe that their prayers make a difference. Because if they believe, really believe, and I'm not talking about giving lip service to an idea, I'm talking about having a conviction that my prayers in fact can make a real difference in the outcome of things. If I can help you to help your people to believe that, they're going to be more inclined to respond to your invitations to pray and your encouragements to pray because you will be able to show them that their prayers do make a difference.

Now, all of us understand that faith has a significant part in our successfulness in prayer. We know that without faith, it is not possible to please God, right? The scripture in Hebrews chapter 11 and verse 6, clearly says *that without faith, it is not possible to please God.* Some amount of faith is required to please Him, although it doesn't say how much faith is required to please Him. At least we think it doesn't say. Therefore, we imagine that however much that amount of faith is that can please God, it's just a little more than we have. We think that some have it, but probably we don't have sufficient faith to please God. But we don't have to be in the dark about how much faith it takes to please God, because in this very scripture, it tells us exactly how much faith is required to please God.

It simply says they that come to God must believe that He is. Now that's a conviction. So that if you can firmly say with conviction, I believe God is, you in fact do have faith, because that's foundational. If you can say, God is, and say that with conviction, you in fact have enough faith to please God. *For they that come to God must believe that he is.*

Now you have that much faith, don't you? Every person who is a member of your church has that much faith, but the kind of faith they hear people talking about is faith that seems to be far superior to that. That it's some kind of faith that reaches way out beyond that level, and since I don't know if I have that other amount... We're talking now about the kind of faith that it takes to please God.

God is not going to answer the prayers of people that do not please him for the most part, unless it is a repentant prayer asking God to forgive us of our wrongdoing. The second part of that statement is that they not only must believe that God is, they must also believe that God is a rewarder of them that diligently seek Him. And I promise you that most of the people in your church will say, "I believe God is, and I believe God rewards those who diligently seek Him." So, that is the fundamental level of faith that is required to please God and anyone with even that amount of faith can pray effectively, if they will pray.

Now faith is like a seed and it's planted in the soil of our souls. Remember that Paul says in the 12th chapter of the book of Romans that God has given to all of us *the measure of faith*. Each one of us who are believers have that fundamental measure of faith, that foundational amount of faith. It's like seed that's planted in the soil of our soul. It has the potential to grow and develop, mature and produce fruit in our lives. But all of us have lived long enough to know that even though there may not be anything wrong with the seed, that seed is not always planted in the same kind of soil.

## Four Kinds of Soil

Of the four kinds of soil that Jesus identified in the parable in the gospel of Matthew, only one of the four kinds of soil was designated as good soil. Then of the good soil, He said it did not produce the same amount of fruit, some 30, some 60, some 100 fold, which says that even though the soil may be good, it does not necessarily mean that faith is going to grow at the same rate in all of our lives, primarily, because we are not all planted in the same kind of atmosphere. There are situations that are conducive to the growth and development of fruit that faith has the power to produce. Then, there are those that are not dwelling in the kind of atmosphere, situations under which faith grows and matures and develops. So in your church, there are all different levels of faith. Some have the potential to produce 100 fold, others, even though they are good soil, do not have that potential. They will never produce more than 30 fold, even though they're good soil and it's good seed and everything may be generally good, yet some produce more than others.

I discovered a long time ago that one of the greatest frustrations of pastoral ministry is trying to get 30 fold soil producing 100 fold. It just doesn't work that way. I need to be totally satisfied that there's good soil and good seed that will never produce any great harvest, but it's good soil and it's good seed and it's real faith that is in their heart, but some are not going to produce as much as others. We'll just have to get used to that and be willing to allow the Lord to do whatever He wants to do in the lives of people.

So you have to understand that faith is there. It is taking root in our life and it does have the potential to grow. Yet it does not grow at the same rate in good soil. It does not have the potential to always produce 100 fold.

Some people's faith grows rather slowly. It grows kind of slowly. It doesn't really produce very quickly and that's all right, but it is faith and it is growing and it does have the potential and will produce. But the problem, one of the basic problems with all this is that just as faith is planted in our heart as a gift from God and has the potential to grow, if that were all of the story, it would be wonderful. But it's not the end of the story, because just as sure as all of us have the measure of faith, we all also have a measure of doubt. You won't ever deal with this problem of doubt by denying that it exists, or by saying if you confess it, it'll be a bad confession and you'll get more of it.

Well, I want to just deal with things right up front, the way they really are, because I haven't found that there is very much of a profit in simply looking at a situation and seeing it clearly and then denying that it exists. I want to find out what the answer is, don't you? Because if I can help my people, if I can cause them to see that they do have faith that it is growing in their lives, and that they also have a measure of doubt that did not come from God, nor did it necessarily come from the devil.

You were not born with it. Little babies trust totally and completely. They are not born with doubt in them. Doubt is the product, the result of living in this world because it is the product of our experiences. We learn that things are not the way we thought they were. Sometimes we learn they are not the way we were told they were.

If I'm trying to build people's faith, by telling them only a part of the truth, they will have the disappointment of experiencing the exact opposite of what they were told. Rather than their faith growing, it will diminish. Doubt will take over in their lives.

Now I might be preaching a sermon that is emphasizing what God does in response to faith, and it may really have a positive effect in the lives of people. And because I cannot preach all of the gospel in one sermon, people may get the wrong idea because there's also another truth that will balance out that positive truth that will help people to get a more realistic view of life the way it really is.

Yes, all of us have the potential to doubt and all of us in fact do have a great deal of doubt more at times than at others. Usually I can tell you, it is not in the heart. It is in the head. Almost always doubt is a product of the mind, the head, not the product of the heart. For my head can be questioning all kinds of things, struggling with many doubts that are in my head while in my heart, I can say with absolute confidence, God is, and God can. So there's not really anything wrong with the faith that is in my heart. It is just that at times, the doubt that is in my mind can overcome and take control of my life and actually override the faith that is in my heart. I'm not then in those times dominated by my faith that is in my heart. I am dominated by the doubt that is in my head.

This is where much of the struggle in our Christian life is. It is being able to overcome the doubts that come to our head, which are the result of experiences we have had or we have seen others have in the world. We were told that it is God's will to heal everyone every time, and so we prayed for a sick mother, our father, our sister, our brother, our daughter, our friend. We prayed earnestly with that understanding that it was God's will to heal them and they were not healed. In fact, they died. You've had an experience like that, haven't you? All the time people were saying, but it's God's will for them to live. It's God's will for them to get well, therefore, if they die, I have to then find out who is to blame for all this because it couldn't be God.

Usually I end up believing it was probably the pastor because he should have had faith or I might blame some member of the board, the elders that they didn't have faith. Finally, I'll come to believe that maybe I didn't have any faith, and ultimately that is one that really I have difficulty struggling through because I know there's some lack here because all the teachers have said, "It's always God's will to heal in every circumstance." Therefore, if they were not healed, it must be we failed rather than it might not possibly have been the will of the Lord in this case.

So we don't seem to know how to balance out that the fact that God does heal, but sometimes chooses for His own reasons not to do so. That's not difficult for me to believe or understand because the better I know the nature and the character of God, the more easily it is for me to understand that God gets glory out of things I seem to feel are defeats. God wins victories when I thought the victory was lost, for God is working in us and through us both to will and to do His own good pleasure. But you see, there has been misunderstandings of a lot of vital promises in the word of God. They have gone unexplained by most of us who are in the ministry, and we, for fear of hurting someone's faith, do not tell them the truth about certain things.

# Anything

Let's take, for instance, the verse of scripture in the gospel of John chapter 14 and verse 13, where the scripture said that Jesus said *whatsoever you ask the father in my name that will I do that the father may be glorified in the son*. Whatsoever you ask. Then He said, *if you shall ask anything in my name*, next verse says, *if you shall ask anything in my name, I will do it*. Now that seems straightforward to me. That doesn't seem like there's anything there to question. If Jesus said anything, He meant anything. I've heard some very wonderful teachers say anything means anything, but it doesn't, and we know that. I mean, we know that without any real deep theological explanation, because it does not mean your secretary. It does not mean a pornographic magazine store.

## Anything Does Not Mean Everything

It does not mean *anything*. It does not mean *everything*. It is a qualified anything. We all understand that if we stop and think about it. But if we leave people the idea that anything means everything, they are certain to be disappointed or they will ask for things that God knows they can't have.

It is true we are teachers. The people are depending on us. We are pastors. We cannot build false expectations, unrealistic expectations in the lives of people, because there are some verses in the scripture that seem to indicate God would do anything we ask Him, anything. The word "anything" is qualified by the nature and the character of God.

I'll give you an illustration that you'll not ever forget, that'll help you to understand that *anything does not mean everything*. It just doesn't mean everything. Now, Dale, I don't know him very well, except I've met him here, but let's say Dale is working for one of these farmers on one of these beautiful farms out here in Pennsylvania.

## To Move the Hand of God?

He's working. He's been working for this farmer for a long time, and one day the farmer says, "Now, Dale, I'd like to have you take the truck and some posts and wire and go build a fence from the Southeast corner of that back acreage to the Northeast corner."

And so Dale loads up all of the materials, the wire, the posts and all, and gets ready to go build a fence as he was instructed to do. Just before he leaves the farmer that he's been working for and trusts says to him, "Now, Dale, if you need *anything* just give me a call on the radio there in the pickup and I'll get it out to you as quickly as I can." So Dale gets out on the backside of the field and he starts building fence and he begins to think now, "You know, the boss said, 'If I need anything, all that I have to do is get on the radio and give him a call.' So what I think I'm going to do is give him a call. He did say *anything*. He did say anything now. So I'm going to give him a call."

Dale gets on the radio and makes contact with the farmhouse and gets the boss on the radio. Dale says, "Boss, you remember saying just before I left to come out here and build this fence, that if I need *anything* that you'd get it out to me as quickly as you could?

"Well, sure, Dale, I remember that. What do you need Dale?"

"Now, Boss, you did say *anything*. Didn't you?"

"Well sure. Dale, what do you need?"

"Well, I need a new car."

Well now, did the boss' anything include the car or was he saying anything that it takes to do what I've commissioned you to do, I will provide for you?

So we've got to understand that *anything* that we read in the scripture do not always apply to *everything*. If we allow our people to go under the illusion that it does, they're certainly building for a disappointment that may not help their faith. In fact, it may destroy their faith. Unrealistic expectations are big faith destroyers. In fact, they build tremendous doubts.

Let me give you an example of a person. Before I go there though, let me just say that practically every person listed in this faith chapter of the Bible had his own personal round with doubt, read them.

## Bout with Doubt

Abraham certainly had his round with doubt. Moses had his round with doubt. David had his round. You look at all of these. How about Elijah? He certainly had his bout with doubt. Everybody said, "Yes, but that's Old Testament stuff. You get in the New Testament, well, it'll be different."

Well, let's look at one that we call John the first Baptist. You remember John the first Baptist? Well, John, you see, was a tremendous man of God. There is no question about that in his generation, Jesus said, *there was no one like him.* He was certainly a man committed to his mission and he knew who Jesus was from his mother's womb. For when Mary, pregnant with Jesus walked into the house of Elizabeth, John literally leapt in his mother's womb.

## John the Baptist

He was full of the Holy Spirit from his mother's womb. He was able to say there's one coming after me, who is mightier than me. He is going to baptize you with the Holy Ghost and fire, and He knew the one he was talking about was none other than his cousin, Jesus. He knew that.

When Jesus finally appeared one day as he was baptizing people in the waters of Jordan confessing their sins, he lifted up his voice and cried out, *There, look behold, that's the lamb of God. He's going to take away the sins of the world.* He knew Jesus' mission. He knew who He was, the Lamb of God, the promised Messiah. John knew that. But if that were not enough, at the baptism of Jesus by John in the waters of Jordan, the scriptures say that the heavens opened and John saw the spirit of God descending upon and lighting upon Jesus as a dove and heard the voice of God from heavens saying, *This is my beloved son in whom I am well pleased.*

Has anyone ever had a greater revelation of Jesus than that? Not me. I've had a wonderful revelation of the Lordship and the divinity of the Lord Jesus Christ, but I've never had anything that equals what John talked about. But later in John's life, he reached the point where he began to doubt that revelation to the point that one day he sent two of his disciples to say, "Are you really the one? Or, should we look for another?"

So let's just get real here. All of us and all of your people are going to have a *bout with doubt* and it's our business to help them to see that this is normal Christianity. The devil wants doubters to believe that they are responsible for everything that's happening that is bad in the church.

He wants them to believe, in fact, that they are the only one with doubts. He wants you to believe that if you tend to be a doubting Thomas or a doubting Thomasina. He wants you to believe that you are the one, that you're the one that's causing this problem, and that nobody else has that struggle with doubt. It is just you. If he can make you believe it, he has robbed you of any kind of an effectual prayer ministry because he is probably keeping you from praying. Not because that would hinder your prayer, but because it will keep you from engaging in prayer.

What was it that caused John the Baptist after having had such a marvelous experience as John had and such definite convictions about the Lordship of Jesus, what could have caused John to begin to have such a problem with doubt? I believe that it's nothing other than unrealistic expectations.

You see John was antisocial. He was a man who lived in the wilderness for the most part, who ate locust and wild honey, and a man who was a teetotaler. He had never drunk wine in all of his life. He had never had any associations with people who lived a low moral life. He withdrew from them.

But one of the first things he heard about Jesus, when Jesus started his ministry, was that Jesus had not only attended a purely social gathering in Cana of Galilee. If that were not enough, He had turned barrels of water into wine. Boy, John could not handle that.

I mean, he really expected Jesus to be more holy, more withdrawn, more separated, more austere than he had ever been. When Jesus did not live up to John's expectations, suddenly he was overwhelmed with a very real problem of questioning the revelation that he had received.

So, when these disciples came and asked Jesus in John's behalf, "Are you really the one or should we look for another?" Jesus, I believe, with a bit of a smile on His face said, *Go tell John the blind see, the deaf hear, the dumb speak, the paralytics are walking. The dead are raised.* By the way, He is saying, *Tell John, blessed is that person who is not offended in me.*

We've got to learn not to be offended when God answers the prayer of someone we believe is less holy than we are. I'll never forget the lady whose husband was not a very committed Christian. She had been suffering from a very severe migraine headache all day. She was the holy one in the family, the spiritual one, the one who spent hours in prayer. Her husband, who was not a very committed Christian, walked in and she complained of this migraine she'd had all day. He walked over and said, "Heal her Jesus." Immediately, her head was well and she got angry. How can you do that God? You've answered his prayer, and I've been crying unto you all day long. The Lord has to sometimes show us that we are viewing things differently than He does.

John the Baptist had to understand that Jesus might not live up to his expectations, but He was doing His Father's will. We need to quit measuring one another. We need to quit grading one another. We need to recognize God's calling upon one another's lives, and if a person doesn't measure up nor conform to my doctrinal position, it could be I'm wrong. It could be he's wrong. It could be we're both wrong. How can that be? Because God is probably not nearly as concerned about doctrinal positions as we are. He probably wouldn't spend any time arguing about them, and if we get close to Him, we probably won't either.

I'm just going to be thankful for how God uses whatever and whomever He uses. God has hit some mighty licks with crooked sticks. Hasn't He? We've all experienced that. He's even hit some pretty good licks through me. I know if He can do that through me, He surely must be able to do it through somebody else. Because if I had a different attitude than that, I would certainly be setting myself in a position where God could not in any sense, bless my life or work through me for He resists the proud. He gives grace to the humble in spirit, to the one who says, "Lord, I know, I can't do anything. I know I'm not worthy, but I believe God is, and I believe God can. I know I have a lot of doubts Father. I know I have a lot of doubts in my mind about things. I don't understand how things work, but I know *God is, and I know God can, and I'm going to pray that He will."*

Somebody said, "Yes, but that was before the day of Pentecost. When you get full of the Holy Ghost, then that's different. I mean, for then all doubt is gone. Then we pray with perfect faith because we can speak in tongues." Well, I wish it were that way, but experience reveals that it is not that way.

# The Church

12th chapter of Acts opens with this statement: Herod killed James with the sword and he held Peter in prison intending to do the same to him after the days of unleavened bread. And if you don't think shock waves went through the church at Jerusalem when James was killed, you don't understand human nature. Because I'm totally convinced that the church fully expected that he would be delivered. Precedent had already been established. Apostles had already been delivered supernaturally. When they got in jail, angels came and led them out of prison. They were so sure of that, that there's a question as to whether or not they even prayed about it. Because they really, and if you've been looking for a positive confession, you would've heard it in Jerusalem.

They would've said when James was arrested, "Oh, he'll be out. Don't worry about it. He'll be out in a day or two. You know what happened when Peter and John were in jail back there? God let him out. James will be out in a few days. Don't worry." And he was - cold dead.

That they did not expect. Shock waves went through the church for Peter is also in jail, and they've already learned of the intention of Herod to put him to death.

They began to try to figure out what to do in view of the critical circumstance that faced them. Someone thought of calling a prayer meeting. They said, "Let's meet for prayer."

While some perhaps were trying to figure out other things to do for their faith seemed to have let them down. They believed that James was going to be delivered and he was in fact killed. So a prayer meeting was called and they began to pray around the clock day and night.

Now either John Mark had an awful big house or just a few people turned out for the prayer meeting. We know the membership of the church was about 5,000 me, and probably a lot more than that. But someone has suggested, "Well, they had home meetings all over town and maybe there was a lot of people praying."

Well, I'll try to give them the benefit of the doubt, but knowing human nature. I'm almost sure that that was the extent of the prayer meeting. What was happening at John Mark's house, but we'll not despise the days of small things. Maybe the number was not great, but they were there praying. They were there asking God to deliver the apostle Peter, and the scripture said they were doing this night and day.

## To Move the Hand of God?

Prayer was made without ceasing unto God by the church for him as two or three days passed. In the middle of the night an angel came, shook Peter awake, got him up, chains fell off, and doors swung open. He found himself outside the prison and discovered that he was not dreaming or having a vision, that he was really wide awake, and that he had been delivered from the prison supernaturally.

Knowing of the prayer meeting going on at John Mark's house, I'm sure they'd got word to him, he went to John Mark's house as quickly as he could. He began to knock on the gate of the enclosure that surrounded the compound where the house was. Rhoda a servant girl heard his summons, came running to the gate and inquired, "Who is it?"

Peter answered, "It's me. It's Peter."

She got so excited, she forgot to unlatch the gate and ran back into the prayer meeting where she announced to this group of dedicated prayer, "Peter is out there at the gate!

Their response was, "Have you lost your mind?"

That's right. You think they were praying with perfect faith? You think they were praying without doubt? I tell you they were struggling with doubt, but they were praying. They were praying, not with perfect faith, not in the absence of doubt, but in spite of their doubts. They were committed to pray and they prayed until the answer came.

Somebody says, "God's not going to hear you if you doubt."

Well, then we may as well quit. Somebody said, "Well, didn't Jesus say that?"

He said, "Doubt not in your heart."

There's a lot of difference in doubting in your head and doubting in your heart. You cannot stop doubt thoughts running through your mind, but you can keep them from dominating your life. You can't keep them from running through. They're going to be there, and sometimes they set up house in our mind. Somehow they begin to have children, and the first thing you know, you've got a house full of them running around in your head.

And all the time your spirit is saying, "But God is, and God can."

But all these little doubts are running through your mind until they begin to dominate your action and have defeated you from a meaningful prayer experience. Yes, and so you've decided, "Well, I'm such a doubter. Nothing can happen if I pray. I've got too many doubts in my mind. It won't work."

Even if Satan makes you believe that doubt is in your heart, it really isn't. It's up here in your head. We are always talking about the difference of having something in your head and having it in your heart, so let's talk about the doubt.

There's a whole lot of difference about having it in your head than having it in your heart. I believe God is and I believe God can, but my mind may be telling me, yes, but He won't answer your prayers.

And you know what? Now that I've learned that, I just say, "Well, we're going to see, because I'm going to pray. God is, and God can."

"Yes, but you don't know if He will."

"No, and I don't know if He won't. I don't know."

Somebody said, "But you have got to believe God will."

The only problem with that teaching is, it just isn't true. You don't have to believe God will. You just have to believe God can and then you pray that He will.

"You mean God would answer the prayer even if I don't believe God will? I just believe He can."

## The Leper

Well let's see. Let's see if He will. Scripture says concerning that leper that came to Jesus that he said, "Lord, I know if you will, you can make me whole." He said, "I don't know if you will or not, but I know you can."

I don't have any doubt about that Jesus said, "Well, that's good enough for me. You know, if you believe I can, I will."

## Imperfect Faith at Ninevah

Listen, that whole bunch of people at Nineveh prayed with an imperfect faith. They said, "It may be God will hear us. We don't know if He will or not. It may be that he'll hear us and we're going to pray and we're going to see."

You mean, you could get an answer if you just said, "God may hear me?"

"Certainly, if you pray."

"You mean even if my faith isn't perfect? Even if I don't know if God will?"

Well, look at the record. Look at what the scripture says. It's a wonderful thing when you can believe and have the revelation that God will do something, and occasionally, we get that kind of revelation and it's a good thing when it happens.

But if you've walked with the Lord very long, you'll know that most often, you're praying without that kind of revelation. <u>You have to believe that God is, and God can, and I'm going to pray that He will, until this</u>

*matter is resolved.* If God chooses not under those conditions to answer my prayer, I will know it must not have been the will of God. God must have had a higher plan, a higher purpose, and I won't have to try to figure out who's to blame. Well, I can live with this kind of teaching, and your people can live with this.

Most of your people today live under tremendous condemnation because they feel that somehow they are the ones that is stopping the moving of God's spirit because their faith is so imperfect. They have not been able to pray with perfect confidence that God will answer their prayer.

What I'm saying is you don't have to pray with perfect confidence that God will. *You only have to believe that God can and commit yourself to praying that He will.* The person who will do that, will see many spectacular answers to prayer. In fact, many more than those who say, "Oh, God's going to do this or God's going to do that," but they don't pray about it. They don't really seek the Lord about it. They say He will, but in their heart, they don't know that for sure at all.

You don't have to know it for sure. You just have to believe God is, and you have to believe, you must believe that God can. Then you set your heart and your mind to say, "I will show my faith by what I do."

Faith is not a mystical thing. Faith is something that can be seen. We put it in the realm of the mystical. It's not mystical. Jesus said you can see it. Some people came to him on one occasion and they had a paralytic friend that they wanted to get into the presence of the Lord in the hope that He would be healed because they knew Jesus had that kind of power. When they got their paralytic friend to the place where Jesus was, they found so many people inside and outside the house that they couldn't even get close.

They made a decision to go up on top of the house and break through the roof and let their paralyzed friend down into the presence of the Lord. Now it's not a small thing to get a paralyzed man on a roof, but they got him up there. It's not easy to break up a roof, but they started breaking up the roof. They determined where the Lord was in the house and they started tearing up the roof.

Can you imagine what's going on down in the room as the dust and debris starts falling down on the people? They start wondering what's going on here and Jesus is trying to teach and He acts as though nothing is happening. Finally, there appear four faces looking down through a little hole and everybody - a lot of people in the house I'm sure, seeing all of this.

Finally, they got the hole big enough. They're now letting down on a sheet, a person, and it's only then the Lord begins to seem to be aware of what's going on. It says, *when He saw their faith*. Well, all He saw was their *action*. What He saw was their *action*.

## Appropriate Action

It doesn't matter what I say. If my saying is not followed by *appropriate action*, my confession is ineffectual and my faith is dead. Any confession of faith must be followed by *appropriate action*, and the *appropriate action is prayer*.

I understand the law of prayer and when I began to put that law into action, I have set up legal grounds for a miracle. I have not guaranteed that a miracle will happen, but I know one thing. The grounds for it have been established. God has the option to do it. He may or may not, because He, after all is God, and He does know in every case, what is best.

What is best and what I think is best can be poles apart, because I'm looking at things from the human time perspective. He's looking at things from the supernatural, divine limitless perspective that only God can view it from.

One day I was saying, "Lord, please tell me why it is I pray about things that do not happen the way I pray?"

Has anyone ever done that besides me? Some of you probably have every prayer that you have ever prayed answered. Well, I'm not one of those though. It would be wonderful if I could say that, but no, I prayed about things and it did not happen that way at all. In fact, it happened exactly opposite of the way I was praying. If I didn't have an understanding about some things, I might tend to be discouraged.

But one day I was asking the Lord, "Tell me why. Why is that Lord? I teach people on prayer. They all want to know the answer to that question. I'd like to have some kind of a reasonable and logical and scriptural answer for that."

How many are getting tired of clichés and verses of scripture quoted out of context to try to deal with real problems? I'm sick of that. I never did like that very much. I believe there are some real answers to real questions and the real answers are not some little cliché or some verse of scripture grabbed up out of context to try to make it apply to a given situation. Maybe it does, maybe it doesn't, but I never had the answer to that until one morning while I was praying.

God began to show me why it is that I pray about something that obviously is the kind of thing God has done in the past, so it is not contrary to His nature, nor would it be that He would have to act out of character to do it, but yet He chose not to do it. God began to show me, and here's how He did it. He said clearly to me that morning, "The law of relativity operates in the spiritual realm the same as in the physical realm."

## Law of Relativity

You said, "Well, that sure doesn't mean much to me."

Well at the moment, instantly, it didn't mean that much. But as quick as I thought about what the Lord was saying, I understood it completely. Because the law of relativity, to put it simply, indicates that *everything in the universe is related, that nothing is happening in a vacuum.* I mean, everything. If there's movement at this point, there's movement all the way down the line.

So what the Lord was saying, when you're praying about a matter over here, what I do here is going to affect things all the way through the chain, until it gets all the way over here. And sometimes what you're asking me to do at this point, can't be done the way you want it done because of the way it's going to affect something here that I'm doing. So you have to be willing and ready to do things in my way to accomplish my ultimate will and my plan.

I suddenly remembered Paul's scripture. It just came to me. The verse out of the 8th chapter of Romans verse

28, where he said, *All things work together*. They are not working separately, and for me to insist upon my will at a certain point is only to indicate my lack of understanding of God's total plan.

I must be willing oftentimes to let it go by simply saying, "Thy will be done."

I know we're hearing an awful lot said about specific prayers. If you're going to pray for a car, tell God the brand and the color and the kind of upholstery, because until you have outlined all the details, God will not respond to that prayer. The Lord may have dealt with someone that way and maybe even dealt with you that way, but do not consider that you're ready to write a book. Because God dealt with you that way that time, does not indicate that that is a precedent that has been established for all people in all times. That is not the general teachings of the word of God.

Maybe He'll want you to do that sometime. If He does, of course, it's the right thing to do. But don't preach that as a doctrine to tell everybody that the only way and the only reason you haven't got your prayers answered is because you haven't been specific enough.

Your people need to know that they have sufficient faith to pray effectually. You've got to teach them that. You can't keep hammering on the fact that it's going to take faith, much more faith than we all have because you see there is no power in faith and there is no power in prayer. The power is in Him.

I don't want to get us thinking that if we can learn to pray just right, we can have anything or if we can get our faith just right, we can have anything. That is a misapplication of truth. No, I'm not going to tell you that. I will tell you if you will pray, believing God is and believing God can, you will establish the conditions under which God has the option to do miracles and many times He will. Many times He will do exactly what you're asking Him to do because He put that desire in your heart that it might be satisfied and that you might know that God has answered your prayer.

But if God doesn't answer that prayer, it is not an indication that there's something wrong with your faith. If you are praying, it is an indication that God may be doing some other things that this doesn't quite fit into at this point in time.

Well, I've got enough faith to pray. How about you? I believe God is.

**Let's say it. I believe God is.**
**And I believe God can.**
**And I'm going to pray that God will.**

I'm going to keep praying until the answer comes whether it's the one I want or not. Hallelujah, let's praise the Lord. Thank you Lord.

## *In Summation*

The following seven powerful principles of prayer are threaded throughout Pastor Willhite's teachings and podcasts:

1. God operates by Divine law and established principle.
2. Things and situations will follow the natural course of action unless there is a reason for them to be otherwise.
3. Prayer justifies God's supernatural intervention into any given situation.
4. God has a Divine will about anything that matters in the universe.
5. I will not allow the doubt in my mind to dominate the faith in my heart.
6. If you have enough faith to pray, you have enough faith to move the hand of God.
7. It is not that we are waiting on God, but God is waiting for us to come in agreement with His will and speak it in our prayers.

## National Call to Prayer

If you would like to receive daily prayer alerts from National Call to Prayer, please use this link:

http://www.nationalcalltoprayer.org

## *One Final Thought...*

*If you have purchased this book on Amazon and it makes a difference in your life ... please consider writing a review to encourage others in their search for answers.*

## Recommended Reading

***Law of Prayer*** –B. J. Willhite

***Why Pray?*** - B. J. Willhite

***How Much Faith Does it Take to Move the Hand of God?*** - B. J. Willhite

***Could You Not Tarry One Hour?*** - *Dr. Larry Lea*

***How to Pray for Your Loved Ones*** – (Also available in Spanish & French) - Dr. Kathy Casto

***There is a Word for Every Storm*** – Dr. Kathy Casto

***The Basics of Hospice Chaplain Ministry*** – Chaplain John Casto

# Notes

## Notes

## To Move the Hand of God?

www.ingramcontent.com/pod-product-compliance
Lightning Source LLC
Chambersburg PA
CBHW071512040426
42444CB00008B/1617